T0120736

THE DILEMMA
OF THE
ADAMS

Pastor Conrad De La Torres

WESTBOW
PRESS®
A DIVISION OF THOMAS NELSON
& ZONDERVAN

Copyright © 2022 Pastor Conrad De La Torres.

All rights reserved. No part of this book may be used or reproduced by any means, graphic, electronic, or mechanical, including photocopying, recording, taping or by any information storage retrieval system without the written permission of the author except in the case of brief quotations embodied in critical articles and reviews.

This book is a work of non-fiction. Unless otherwise noted, the author and the publisher make no explicit guarantees as to the accuracy of the information contained in this book and in some cases, names of people and places have been altered to protect their privacy.

WestBow Press books may be ordered through booksellers or by contacting:

WestBow Press
A Division of Thomas Nelson & Zondervan
1663 Liberty Drive
Bloomington, IN 47403
www.westbowpress.com
844-714-3454

Because of the dynamic nature of the Internet, any web addresses or links contained in this book may have changed since publication and may no longer be valid. The views expressed in this work are solely those of the author and do not necessarily reflect the views of the publisher, and the publisher hereby disclaims any responsibility for them.

Any people depicted in stock imagery provided by Getty Images are models, and such images are being used for illustrative purposes only.
Certain stock imagery © Getty Images.

Unless otherwise indicated, all Scripture is taken from the King James Version.

Scripture marked (NKJV) taken from the New King James Version®. Copyright © 1982 by Thomas Nelson. Used by permission. All rights reserved.

Scripture quotations marked (ESV) are from the ESV® Bible (The Holy Bible, English Standard Version®), copyright © 2001 by Crossway, a publishing ministry of Good News Publishers. Used by permission. All rights reserved.

ISBN: 978-1-6642-5204-2 (sc)
ISBN: 978-1-6642-5206-6 (hc)
ISBN: 978-1-6642-5205-9 (e)

Library of Congress Control Number: 2021924848

Print information available on the last page.

WestBow Press rev. date: 12/18/2021

CONTENTS

❖

To my beautiful wife, Patricia, who has been my life's companion and encourager, all while raising two young children while I was doing six years in prison. I thank God for her strength and wisdom that can only come from Him. I also dedicate it to my daughter, Monique, and my son, Conrad, who had to endure growing up without a dad for six years. I thank God for the awesome man and woman they have turned out to be. Monique and her husband, Steve, have blessed us with three grandchildren—Mia, Drew, and Logan. Conrad and his wife, Stephanie, have blessed us with one son, Dominic. May the Lord let the seed of His Word produce fruit in their lives forever.

I would also like to thank my other family members and my Christian family at Fusion Church in Homestead, Florida. I will not mention all their names because there are just too many to list. The last thing I would want to do is sadden any of these precious family and church members by leaving their names out. Thank you for your faithfulness and service. Thank you for sticking with Patty and me and being there for us in the good and the bad times. Thank you for your love and support. I am excited to see what the Lord has in store for us in the future.

FOREWORD

I t is with great pleasure that I write this foreword to my pastor's first book. I have read the book twice and enjoyed it both times. I'm deeply honored that out of many possible candidates to write this foreword, my friend and pastor, Conrad De La Torres, chose me. There have been few men in my sixty years who I have considered my friend. Outside of my father, this is the only other man in the world I would trust with my life. Many who know Pastor De La Torres have eagerly waited for this book. I feel blessed to be under this man's teaching. There are but a few men of God who are great preachers—and even fewer who are also great teachers. Well, here is a man of God who is a superb preacher, teacher, servant, and, in the tradition of Peter, a fisherman of both man and fish. This book is of great value to everyone, regardless of spiritual level: the mature Christian; the new in Christ; and most importantly, to bring the nonbeliever to Christ.

In the more than ten years in which Conrad has been my pastor, I have seen God use him mightily in the work of His kingdom. There have been instances where he has shared the Gospel with people I know. I wondered if some thought I had revealed things about them to him. His drive, dedication, and passion for the Gospel of our Lord, Jesus Christ, is inspiring. This is why his first book carries so much weight for me. This is not someone teaching you out of mental knowledge. This is a man teaching you things that God taught him (as you will read) in the fiery furnace, when he had nothing but God.

I hope once you read this book, you will be moved to share it with all of your family and friends. If you care about their spiritual well-being, regardless of their level, they will be well served by the teachings in this book. I truly hope my friend and pastor writes many more books like this one. There will always be at least two copies in my library—one to cherish and one to share.

—Silvio Gonzalez, retired businessman, current farmer,
   author of *Let There Be Light*

ACKNOWLEDGMENTS

First, I want to thank my Lord and Savior, Jesus Christ, without whom I would have no hope of heaven, and I do not know how I would have made it on earth. I am a living picture of the prodigal son. God, in His mercy, has not only saved me but has also allowed me to serve Him. Wow! Who would have guessed?

I would also like to thank my brother in Christ Jeff Friend for his help in editing this book. May the Lord continue to use his gifts to bless many.

INTRODUCTION

I was born in Cuba, the second of six siblings born to Conrado and Fidelina De La Torres. I have three sisters, Carrie, Marianna, and Barbara, and two brothers, Jesus and Angel. We lived on the Playa De Guanabo, a beautiful beach on the east of Cuba, until our escape in 1963.

I remember playing in the *trincheras* (trenches) that the Cuban soldiers (Milicianos) had built on the beach in preparation for an invasion from the United States.

My father had been involved in anti-Castro activities and consequently was wanted by the Castro regime. He would have been put in front of a firing squad had they found him. He had served in the navy during the Batista government.

My father captained a boat for a wealthy man who was planning to escape from Cuba with his family. He offered my father a way out. The man promised passage to America for my father and our family if my father captained the boat to get there.

I was seven years old, and the few memories that have remained flicker in and out of my mind and then evaporate like a dream. I do remember my father having a little store called a *ciosco*.

One thing I will never forget is the night we escaped. There was a lot of rushing and running around. My mom was trying to herd her six small children, ranging in age from ten years old to only a few months old. My mother must have been so scared. I remember going through the woods and being told repeatedly to be quiet because the militia men had apparently been informed of our escape and were searching for us.

When we thought the men had left, we finally made our way to the boat and met up with the man and his family. We took off in the middle of the night and were headed for the United States of America.

During the upheaval and distress, something unthinkable happened that almost caused the demise of everyone on board. The person responsible for the survival provisions had left everything back on land. There were twenty-three people on a twenty-three-foot boat with no food and no water. I am sure that there were at least six children. After three harrowing days, we arrived at a private dock in Marathon, Florida. I have never stopped thanking God for getting us through that!

I wish my father and mother were alive to see this book. As I write *The Dilemma of the Adams*, I can only imagine the incredible dilemma they faced, as they had to choose between staying in Cuba and having our family live in an oppressed communist country or risk all our lives at sea.

I thank God for giving them the courage and resolve to choose freedom. I thank God He allowed us to come to the greatest country on the face of the earth—America!

Beloved, we all experience great dilemmas, times when we are forced to make decisions that could go one way or the other, neither of which is good. There are even times when we are faced with decisions that could have serious consequences, even eternal ramifications. In this book, you will read about the greatest dilemmas that have ever been experienced on this earth, and with the greatest of eternal ramifications.

May the Lord use this book to teach us how to handle the dilemmas in our lives and to understand in greater depth the dilemma of the Adams.

I humbly ask you to please stop now for a moment and pray that the Lord will reveal not only His heart but also my heart to you as you read.

CHAPTER ONE

THE BIBLE

B eloved, will you believe me when I tell you that the Bible, if you take it in its simplest form, is about two men, in two gardens, in love with two women, facing two dilemmas, and having to make two decisions?

Sin killed them both! Sin killed the first Adam in disobedience, and sin killed the last Adam in obedience.

The Bible—Basic Instructions Before Leaving Earth. I remember the first time I read or heard that. I said, "Wow, how true! The human being's owner's manual."

For a while, I worked as a car salesman at a Toyota dealership in Homestead, Florida. One of the first things I was told was to *never* deliver a car without an owner's manual. Later, I came to understand why. I cannot tell you the number of times I have found myself reaching in the glove box and looking for the owner's manual to help me know where something is or how to work something in my car or truck.

In the same way, we can go to the Bible and find the answer to any and every question—not only answers but also the guidance we need as we go through life. And most importantly, it shows us how to receive and prepare for life after death. I was almost going to write "how to prepare for eternal life," but I stopped myself because there is a big misconception about the word *eternal*.

What most people do not seem to know or understand is that we are all eternal beings. We were created in the image of God, in that we are eternal. In other words, our spirits will never cease to exist.

Receiving Jesus as your Savior does not determine whether you live forever or not. You will live forever in one place or another. Receiving Jesus as Savior just determines where you will spend that eternity. You will either be with Him in heaven or you will be forever separated from Him in a place the Bible calls hell (Matthew 10:28).

Mot preachers hesitate to preach that anymore, but it is the absolute truth. Another way of putting it is this: if you are born once, you will die twice. If you are born twice, you will die once (or never experience physical death at all if you are caught up in the Rapture).

I will explain the Rapture in another chapter.

I believe with all my heart that what some people fail to see is that the Bible is *alive*!

There are books on just about every topic you can think of. Books that claim they can help you change not only the way you think but also how you behave. Books that boast they can help you become a better person, or make you a better speaker, or show you how to make and influence friends. Books to encourage you and make you feel better. Books to teach you just about any trade or anything you want to learn. Or maybe you just want to get lost in some fantasy and forget about life for a while. Well, there are plenty of books for that too.

But there is only one book that can transform you. And that, my friend, is the Bible, the Living Word of God. It will enter you as some invisible spiritual katana, cut you to the quick, and reveal you to yourself. It is *alive*!

And nothing scares us more than us!

The Bible will show you some things about yourself you never knew. And once inside you, it can heal, repair, change, and, if you let it, even transform you into a brand-new you, a living you (2 Corinthians 5:17).

Please note that the Bible is not necessarily a book on theology, history, science, or any other topic. In fact, it was not written to explain God. It just starts off with the emphatic statement, "In the beginning God" (Genesis 1:1).

It is a book God gave humanity that reveals His plan and purpose on planet Earth. Like I said before, it's the human being's owner's manual.

God used different men from different times and with different personalities, backgrounds, and positions to pen His Word. He used kings such as David and Solomon, statesmen like Daniel and Nehemiah, and priests like Ezra. He used Moses, who God had placed in the palace of Pharaoh, that he might learn the wisdom of Egypt, and prophets like Isaiah, Ezekiel, and Zechariah.

God used a shepherd named Amos and a tax collector named Matthew. He used fisher folks like Peter, John, and James, and even Paul, a Pharisee whom God threw off his horse to get his attention. Oh, and let's not forget Doctor Luke.

These men wrote from many different places, from the wilderness of Sinai to the courts of the temple, and from a prison in Rome to the isle of Patmos in the Aegean Sea.

God's Spirit moved them and through them, giving us sixty-six books, thirty-nine in the Old Testament and twenty-seven in the New Testament.

It was written in three languages—Hebrew, Greek, and some Aramaic—and on three different continents.

You would have thought that the Bible would have turned out to be theological soup, compiled by all these different men, most of whom did not live in the same era, much less know one another. But as you read it, you soon notice that these books fit like a hand in a glove and that there is a beautiful progression of revelation and doctrine in it.

It has blue-to-red illumination, which I will explain later.

The language of the Bible is threefold: figurative, symbolic, and literal. The figurative is explained by the context, the symbolic is explained either in the context or somewhere else in the scriptures, and the rest should be taken literally.

We need to take the Bible literally until otherwise asked. We need to let the Bible say what it wants to say without allegorizing or spiritualizing its meaning.

I hear people all the time trying to justify sin or some wrong decision in their lives by saying, "This is what this verse means to me," or "This is how it speaks to me," or "This is how I interpret that verse."

While I am glad that they are at least reading the Word, we do not only need to understand what we are reading; we also need to read it in context. We need to find what God intended it to mean when He wrote it, not what we think it means. What we think it to mean amounts to nothing if it is not what God meant it to say.

One of the biggest mistakes I see in the body of Christ is that we tend to take things that were written to Israel and cram them down the church's throat.

Please understand me when I say that while all of the Bible was written *for* us, not all of the Bible was written *to* us.

Part of it is addressed to the Jews, and it applies to the nation of Israel and only to them. Part is written to and about the Gentiles, and part is written to and for the church, the body of Christ.

These are the only three classes of people on earth. Therefore, in the body of Christ, there is and should be no prejudice.

A Jew (in Hebrew, *Yehudi*) comes from the name Judah, which was the name of one of Jacob's twelve sons. By the way, our Lord and Savior Jesus was born into the tribe of Judah. In Revelation 5:5, He is called "the Lion of the tribe of Judah." The original name of the people we now call Jews was "Hebrew," first used in the Torah to describe Abraham (Genesis 14:13).

Judaism is a religion as well as a race and culture. Jews come from all over the world, from many different ethnicities and nationalities. A Gentile is anyone who is not a Jew. The church is made up of both Jews and Gentiles who have received Christ as Savior.

> Give none offence, neither to the Jews, nor to the Gentiles, nor to the church of God. (1 Corinthians 10:32)

The church is not mentioned in the Old Testament. The Old Testament is mostly taken up with the history of one nation—Israel, the Jews.

It is interesting that we like to take the promises written to and for the Jews but don't want anything to do with the curses.

We (the church) tend to take things in the Bible written to and for the Jews, or to others, and claim them for ourselves, which leads to a lot of wrong doctrine and confusion.

For example, suppose that we live in the same house. We share one mailbox. One day, I happen to be downstairs when the mailman delivers the mail. I pick up a letter, open it, and to my surprise, it says, "You have just won $1,000,000." I jump up and almost pass out from the shock and excitement.

But when I take a closer look, the check is made out to you.

I opened your mail by mistake. Now I must tell you that while I am still incredibly happy for you, and you may even decide to bless me with some of your winnings, I cannot cash the check and spend that money. It was not written to me; it was written to you.

There are many examples of this misapplication of scripture I can give you, but I will give you one more from the New Testament.

In the book of Acts, chapter 16, we find Paul and Silas had been thrown in prison in Philippi (a former city in present-day Greece) for preaching the Word of God. The chapter goes on to tell us that at midnight they prayed and sang praises to the Lord, and all the prisoners heard them.

Suddenly there was a great earthquake that shook the very foundation of that prison and opened all the prison doors.

The prison guard, thinking that all the prisoners had escaped, which would have cost him his life for allowing it, was about to kill himself with his sword. But he heard Paul cry out, "Don't hurt yourself, we are all here!"

The prison guard (whose heart I believe was already softened by the Holy Spirit through all the praise and worship) realized that all the prisoners were there. He went in and fell before Paul and Silas, asking them how he could be saved.

Paul tells him, and this is the verse I want to expound on. This is one of the most misused, misquoted verses in the Bible.

Acts 16:31 says, "So they said, 'Believe on the Lord Jesus Christ, and you will be saved, you and your household'" (NKJV).

A few years ago, a precious woman and her children started to attend our church. She had come from what I call a hyper-faith church. So I knew that her mindset (and most of the people who come from that theology) was "Don't confuse me with the facts; my mind is already made up."

She stayed for a while and then moved on to a church that taught what she believed and what she had been wrongfully taught. No wonder brother Paul had to tell Timothy that there was coming a time (it is here!) when people would not want to listen to true doctrine but would search for pastors and teachers who would teach them what they wanted to hear (2 Timothy 4:3).

I was telling one of my young men recently that most people who come in for counseling do not want counsel; they want confirmation. It reminded me of this verse.

A few years later, I ran into this sister at a gym she worked at and I attended. I asked her about her children, and she told me they had gone way off the path of righteousness and that they were living in utter sin. But she said they were saved because God had promised in His Word that she and her whole household would be saved.

It took a couple more years and many conversations before I felt I had the opening to explain that verse to this sister in a way that she would understand it and accept it.

Are the words "Today you and your whole house will be saved" in the Bible? Yes! But it was said to the jailer, not us! And that night, the jailer and all his family were saved (Acts 16:32–33).

I could write another book just on the many verses that we take out of context and cram down the church's throat, leading many to fall away from God and His church because they just do not work. And it is not that they don't work; they do! It is just that they were not written to us.

The epistle of James, for example, is not addressed to the church but to the twelve tribes of Israel.

James, a servant of God and of the Lord Jesus Christ, to the twelve tribes which are scattered abroad, greeting. (James 1:1)

We must not apply to the church what does not belong to it. To do so is to misapply scripture and lead to confusion.

❖

CHAPTER TWO

THE HEAVENS TESTED

Someone said, "A faith that cannot be tested is a faith that cannot be trusted!"

No one knows how much time there was from the creation of the earth until the creation of Adam. The Word simply says, "In the beginning God created the heaven and the earth" (Genesis 1:1).

We will call this time the pre-Adamite earth.

The first test ever to take place occurred in the heavens by a cherub named Lucifer.

In Ezekiel 28, Ezekiel seems to shed some light on this subject. There seems to be a double meaning here. One pertains to the king (human ruler) of Tyre who was condemned for claiming to be God. And the other is that Ezekiel is also referring to the actual fall of the cherub Lucifer from heaven, consequently named Satan, who happened to be the real power behind the king of Tyre.

Moreover the word of the LORD came to me, saying, "Son of man, take up a lamentation for the king of Tyre, and say to him,

'Thus says the Lord GOD: "You were the seal of perfection, Full of wisdom and perfect in beauty."'" (Ezekiel 28:11–12 NKJV)

Did you catch the phrase in verse 12? *The seal* or *the sum* of all beauty and perfection. I don't think mere mortals like us can now, or will ever, really understand this until the day we are translated into perfection ourselves and we know as we are known.

I like to visualize it this way: *the sum* of all beauty and perfection! Take a glass of water and fill it to the brim to where not one more drop can fit in the cup; that is the sum. In other words, please try to understand this: Lucifer could not have been more beautiful. He could not have been more perfect! I believe that he was so beautiful that his beauty caused the other beings to praise God, much like we do here on earth when we gaze at a beautiful sunset, flower, or any of God's incredible creations.

Ezekiel tells us that Lucifer was given the Garden of Eden and that precious stones were his covering.

Thou hast been in Eden the garden of God; every precious stone was thy covering. (Ezekiel 28:13)

You were in the garden in Eden. Apparently, Lucifer was given the Garden of Eden to rule over before Adam was even formed.

I believe that he might have even overseen a pre-Adamite race, not created (if they did exist) in the image of God.

Ezekiel goes on to say that Lucifer walked back and forth on the Holy Mountain of God, amid the fiery stones. Verses 14 and 15:

You were the anointed cherub who covers; I established you; You were on the holy mountain of God; You walked back and forth in the midst of fiery stones. You were perfect in your ways from the day you were created, till iniquity was found in you. (NKJV)

I suggest to you that Lucifer was the first creature to go contrary to his very character. We will deal with that a little later.

Isaiah seems to shed some light on what may have happened when he wrote, speaking of this incredible creature by the name of Lucifer (which, by the way, means Son of the Morning, Shining One, Bearer of Light, or Morning Star):

How you are fallen from heaven, O Lucifer, son of the morning! How you are cut down to the ground, You who weakened the nations! For you have said in your heart: "I will ascend into heaven, I will exalt my throne above the stars of God; I will also sit on the mount of the congregation on the farthest sides of the north; I will ascend above the heights of the clouds, I will be like the Most High." (Isaiah 14:12–14 NKJV)

Have you ever stopped to ask yourself, "How did this *perfect* creature, created by a perfect God and in a perfect world, sin? How did sin ever enter?"

Well, it was birthed in him!

His nature was perfect. We just read it, but let us read it again. "You were perfect in your ways from the day you were created, Till iniquity was found in you" (Ezekiel 28:15 NKJV).

Sin was literally *birthed* in him!

This is how I think it happened. There are probably millions upon millions of angels in heaven, and it is probably the same for every other creature God created.

Astronomers tell us that there are two hundred billion stars just in our Milky Way galaxy alone. And not only that, but our galaxy is also one of twenty-seven galaxies that span three million light-years. This is only a small fraction of this incredible universe, which contains over two hundred billion galaxies.

And it is estimated that each of these galaxies has more than one hundred billion stars. Our minds cannot even comprehend this kind of vastness. And to think that it all came about by the Word of God's power. God said it, and it was (Genesis 1:1).

For He spoke, and it was done; He commanded, and it stood fast. (Psalm 33:9 NKJV)

I think science teaches us that the universe is expanding and that they really do not know why. Well, let me tell them. The Bible teaches us that God's Word will not come back void (Isaiah 55:11).

I like to say that I believe in the big bang theory: God said it, and—*bang*—it was!

The universe is expanding because God's Word is so powerful, so alive, that when He said, "Let there be," it is still out there being! It is still creating!

If I were in the pulpit right now, I would be saying, "Can I get an amen?"

I tell my congregation that if they have the bumper sticker I've seen on the back of many cars and trucks that says, "God said it, I believe it, and that settles it!" they might as well take it off.

It is wrong theology! God said it … and that settles it!

Whether we believe it or not does not change that reality.

I asked my congregation, "How many legs would you say your dog had if you believed his tail to be a leg?"

Of course, most yelled out, "Five!"

To which I replied, "No!" You can call his tail a leg from now to doomsday, and it will never be a leg! The reality is a dog has four legs, and nothing we believe to the contrary will or can change that!

God said it, and it was! And that settles it!

To say that I believe that there are millions, maybe billions, of angels, seraphim, cherubim, and who knows what other creatures there may be is to (I think) cut myself short. Regardless of the number of creatures, the Bible tells us that Lucifer was the "sum of beauty and perfection" of all of God's creation.

Like I said before, Lucifer was given the Garden of Eden to tend and rule. That might have been a race of creatures before Adam, not created in the image of God (we will call them pre-Adamites), that inhabited the earth at the time. This is probably where we get the dinosaur and all the hominids or prehumans that scientists keep telling us (wrongly) are our ancestors.

It was in this garden (Eden) and because of the sum of his beauty and power that sin was birthed and Lucifer decided to overthrow his very Creator.

Imagine Pinocchio given the ability by a fairy to become human. Having received this new form and power, Pinocchio tries to usurp the authority of his creator, Geppetto, and take over the toy store. And not only that, he convinces one-third of all the toys to join him in his takeover.

That, beloved, is exactly what Lucifer did. Please understand that it did not take God by surprise. As a matter of fact, God allowed it. God wanted His heavens tested.

I believe God held court in heaven and allowed Lucifer to give his state of the heavens address, if you will. I think God tested all of heaven and gave Lucifer an opportunity to convince the rest of the creatures in heaven as to why they should follow him and not God.

Maybe he somehow convinced the seraphim that he was not going to make them have to say "Holy, holy, holy" twenty-four hours a day any longer. In Revelation 4:8, it speaks of these creatures standing in front of the throne all day and all night, saying "Holy, holy, holy, Lord God Almighty, Who was and is and is to come!" (NKJV).

One thing we do know is that he caused one-third of the stars (angels) from heaven to fall with him. Now, while there is no verse that says, "A third of the angels fell from heaven," I, and many other students of the Word, have come to the conclusion that it is Lucifer, later called Satan, the book of Revelation is referring to when it says, "Then the fifth angel sounded: And I saw a star (Satan) fallen from heaven to the earth. To him was given the key to the bottomless pit" (Revelation 9:1 NKJV).

In chapter 12, verse 4, Revelation tells us, "His tail drew a third of the stars of heaven and threw them to the earth" (NKJV).

What an incredible picture of the fall of Lucifer. I pray you took special notice of verse 4: *"His tail drew a third of the stars of heaven* and threw them to the earth" (emphasis mine).

In other words, when Satan fell, one-third of God's angelic host followed him. The verse goes on to say, "And the dragon stood before the woman who was ready to give birth, to devour her Child (Jesus) ... who was to rule all nations with a rod of iron. And her Child was caught up (His ascension to heaven in plain view) to God and His Throne" (Revelation 12:4–5 NKJV).

Of course, if you are a student of the Bible, you know that the woman referred to here is none other than the nation of Israel, and her child is Jesus.

Satan did all he could to stop the birth of Jesus. He convinced King Herod to massacre all male children from two years old and younger (Matthew 2:16).

Jesus Himself said when referring to the fall of Lucifer, "And He said to them, 'I saw Satan fall like lightning from heaven'" (Luke 10:18 NKJV).

Since Satan himself is referred to as "a star" in Revelation 9:1, I think it is safe to conclude that "the stars" refer to fallen angels.

What we have here, beloved, is the actual birth of sin before the creation and the fall of Adam. It was birthed in the free will of Lucifer, and so he was consequently thrown out of the third heaven, as per his domain.

Please understand that Satan cannot and does not live in

God's third heaven. I will explain why I say *third* later. He does, however, still have access to it. Of this we can get no clearer picture than the one given to us in the book of Job 1:6–12.

Oh, make no mistake about it! Satan has access to the throne. And he uses that access to accuse us (Christians) before God Himself. You read right! *Us!* Any and every person born again by the blood of Jesus.

But one day, the heavens will rejoice because the devil will be cast down to earth. On that day, all hell will break loose on earth because Satan will know he has just a short while before the Lord deals with him for good (Revelation 12:12).

You may be asking, "Pastor, where did you get the third heaven thing from?" Well, from Paul. In 2 Corinthians 12:2–4, he tells us of an incredible experience he had. He says he was taken to the third heaven and that he really does not know if it was physically or spiritually. Apparently, he saw and heard things so awesome that he was not even allowed to repeat them.

I believe this happened when Paul was stoned and left for dead in Acts 14:19. I think it was here that Paul died and was taken to the third heaven where paradise is.

Having been kicked out of both the third heaven and earth, Lucifer destroyed the pre-Adamite earth with a flood. This flood, according to some scholars, was even worse than Noah's flood. It lasted longer and killed all living things, including vegetation, which did not happen during Noah's flood (Genesis 8:11).

Genesis 1:2 (NKJV) says, "The earth was without form, and void; and darkness was on the face of the deep. And the Spirit of God was hovering over the face of the waters" (caused, some will argue, by Lucifer's flood).

So when God says, "Let there be light," in Genesis 1:3, God starts His six days of restoring the earth and creating new creatures, including man on the sixth day (Genesis 1:26–28).

Many believe that it was Lucifer's flood that caused the dinosaurs to become extinct and all the pre-Adamites to die.

The book of Job says that only He who created them (many, including myself, believe this is referring to the dinosaurs) can bring His sword near them (Job 40:19).

So, God either drew His sword Himself or used Lucifer's flood (if indeed it happened) to get rid of the dinosaurs. We won't know until we get to heaven.

It may also be the reason why we have found fossils of hominids, nonhuman or prehuman, although humanlike creatures. Something to think about and do further research on.

He and his fallen angels now occupy the heavens, and they are the principalities and powers over which Satan rules and whom we are warned about in Ephesians 6:12.

By the way, the spiritual beings called demons may very well be the disembodied spirits of these creatures. Before Adam, I do not think that God had ever made any creature in His likeness. And so, the heavens were tested!

How much time between the creation of the pre-Adamite earth and it becoming formless and void we do not know. Neither do we know how long it continued in that condition. But when the time came, God restored the earth to its habitable state and made it fit for humans. And He did it in six days.

Five times we are told that the living creatures reproduced after their own kind, which means they did not come from one common ancestor. That the Word says man was *created* tells us plainly that we *did not* evolve from apes!

Man was made in the image of God and was not formed from a beast but of the dust of the earth.

Male and female created he them. (Genesis 1:27)

This age or dispensation is called the Edenic Dispensation, or the Dispensation of Innocence.

Now, if you have never heard the term *dispensation*, it is a period in which God deals with humans. God deals with and dispenses His purpose and His plans to humans in different ways, and the form in which God deals with humans is different and progressive in each dispensation.

Please note that there is a difference between an age and a dispensation. An age stands for a period between two great physical changes in the earth's surface, while a dispensation is a moral or probationary period.

For example, this present age began with the flood of Noah, and it will end when Christ returns to earth—not the Rapture but the literal return to earth with ten thousand of His saints (Jude 1:14).

In the book of Exodus, God gave the law to Moses, which ushered in the dispensation of Law. We are living right now under the dispensation of Grace. The next dispensation will be the Messianic Dispensation or the Millennial Kingdom.

Let me share with you a little more about dispensations.

The dispensations are as follows:

1. The Edenic or Dispensation of Innocence
    This dispensation covers the time from the creation of humans to the fall of humans.

2. The Dispensation of Conscience
    This was from the time that humans were expelled from the garden until the dispensation of Law.

    It was a time when humans did whatever they wanted (Genesis 6:5–6).

    This is also when the fallen angels left the heavenlies, their first estate (their proper domain), went to earth, and joined with mortal women, thus producing giants called Nephilim (Genesis 6:1–4).

3. The Dispensation of Human Government
   This dispensation started not too long after the flood. God promises Noah that He will never completely flood the earth again. He gives permission to use animals for food and tells Noah and his family to repopulate the earth. It is here that God establishes the law of capital punishment (Genesis chapters 8 and 9).

   Proverbs 16:18 says, "Pride goes before destruction, And a haughty spirit before a fall" (NKJV).

   In Genesis 11:1–9, the account of the Tower of Babel tells us that after Noah's flood, everyone in the world spoke the same language.

   As the population began to grow, people moved to new areas. A group of people moved to the Plain of Shinar. We know it today as Babylonia or part of Iraq.

   There, they decided to build a tower that would reach to the heavens. They wanted to make a name for themselves, and they did not want to be scattered to other areas of the earth.

   Some scholars think that these people remembered the Great Flood of Noah. Apparently, they did not believe that God would keep his word. They did not believe in the covenant of the rainbow.

   Other scholars think the Babel people thought they could build a tower that reached heaven and somehow become gods—to become equal with God.

   How many lost souls do you know who are trying to get to heaven in some way other than God's way? Beloved, we can never be good enough, powerful enough, smart enough, creative enough, loving enough, or holy enough to become a god and save ourselves.

   How ironic that the scripture says, "But the Lord

came down to see the city and the Tower that the men had built" (Genesis 11:5 NKJV).

Their tower had not reached heaven at all. In fact, God had to come down to see the city.

They had one language, and the plan was for everyone to live in the same place to accomplish great things. But in the end, God reversed their plan and scattered them over all the earth.

This dispensation lasted until God called Abraham.

4. The Dispensation of Promise
    The patriarchs and the affliction of Israel in Egypt as slaves for 430 years until the time of the Exodus all fall into this dispensation.

5. The Dispensation of Law
    This dispensation started with Moses leading the nation of Israel out of the bondage of Egypt and God giving Moses the Law and the blueprints for the Tabernacle (Exodus 19–31). It ended with the death, burial, and resurrection of Jesus the Christ!

6. The Dispensation of Grace
    This dispensation started at the resurrection of Jesus. It is also called the age of grace or the church age.

7. The Millennial Kingdom of Christ
    This is the thousand-year reign of Christ on earth. Satan will be bound (Revelation 20:1–3), and Christ will rule in a theocracy on earth. Satan will be set free for a short time (verse 4) for a final judgment of the people on earth (Revelation 20:7–10), and the old earth and heaven will be

destroyed by fire. Satan will be forever thrown into the lake of fire, and this will usher in eternity.

8. Eternity Future

Now let's get back to Adam.

Adam and Eve were perfect, in perfect union with God, their Creator, and innocent of evil. They had no conscience before the Fall. They were both naked and were not ashamed (Genesis 2:25).

Conscience is knowledge of good and evil, and Adam and Eve did not have this until they had their eyes opened by eating of the fruit of the Tree of the Knowledge of Good and Evil (Genesis 2:17).

❖

CHAPTER THREE

A CREATURE IN THE IMAGE OF HIS CREATOR

I believe that one of the biggest reasons there are so many different denominations, cults, and beliefs, as well as so much confusion, in the body of Christ (the church) is because few really understand the Bible.

For example, if you do not understand what happened in the Garden of Eden, you will never really grasp and understand what happened in the Garden of Gethsemane or the rest of the Bible.

Why is Jesus called the second Adam?

It is my intention and prayer that with God's help and the guidance of the Holy Spirit, I will answer some of these questions in this book.

Many times, I sat down to write and never followed through because of my feelings of inadequacy. I personally do not think I can write a letter, much less try to explain the deep, incredible things of God.

I've had the title to my book in my head for many years. I told many people that I was going to write it. But it was not until my brother and friend Silvio Gonzalez published his book, *Let There Be Light*, that I was not only convicted to write it but, more than that, inspired.

Someone well said that the Old Testament is the New Testament concealed, and the New Testament is the Old Testament revealed.

Everything in the Old Testament is there to point us to Jesus. If you miss that, you will miss the whole counsel of God.

In the book of Genesis, we read that God formed man out of the dust of the earth and literally breathed His life (Spirit) into the new form He had fashioned. It became alive, and He called it man.

Please understand that God had never breathed Himself, His Spirit, into any other creature He had ever created before Adam, even beings like the seraphim, which the book of Isaiah tells us are six-winged beings that fly around the throne of God, crying, "Holy, holy, holy" (Isaiah 6:1–3).

Other creatures or beings the Bible speaks about are the cherubim. From what we read in Ezekiel 10:14, they seem to only have four wings, and they have four faces. They appear in several of the books of the Bible, including Ezekiel, Genesis, 1 Kings, and Revelation.

Then there are angels, which, according to the book of Hebrews, are ministering spirits.

Sometime after Satan was kicked out (and we do not know how long), God decided to create a creature unlike any He had ever created. God decided to make a creature in His own likeness.

Please know that every other creature God ever created was a species unto itself. By that I mean that there are no momma angels and daddy angels that have baby angels. They neither marry nor are given in marriage (Mark 12:25). They are like the snowflakes that God asked Job to consider when He asked him, "Have you entered the treasury of the snow, Or seen the treasury of the hail" in Job 38:22 (NKJV).

By the way, it was only after the invention of the microscope that we discovered that no two snowflakes are alike. They are a species unto themselves—a miracle, a masterpiece of beauty that God in His utter love and perfection gave us so that we can grasp (just a little) of not only His creative power but also His unsearchable love for us, the only creatures created in His image.

God, speaking of Jesus before He was born as the child Jesus, said He was called the Word (John 1:1). "In the beginning was the Word, and the Word was with God, and the Word was God." And if you jump down to verse 14, it says, "And the Word became flesh." In other words, the Word became Jesus!

Speaking to the Word, "Then God said, 'Let Us make man in Our image, according to Our likeness'" (Genesis 1:26a NKJV).

Genesis 2:7 gives us a little more insight into the divine creation of Adam. "And the LORD God formed man of the dust of the ground and breathed into his nostrils the breath of life; and man became a living being."

Adam was the first creature to be made in the likeness of God. Just as God is a triune being (Father, Son, Holy Spirit), Adam was created as a triune being—body, soul, and spirit. God then gives him charge of all of Eden (Genesis 1:26b).

Everything on earth was placed under Adam's care. The Lord God had formed every beast of the field and every bird of the air and brought them to Adam for him to name, but God had not formed another creature in the likeness of Adam. God had not formed another man from the ground (Genesis 2:18–20).

Yet the Lord Himself had said that it was not good for Adam to be alone. Notice that God never said that Adam was lonely, only that it was not good for him to be alone.

God not only knew how Adam felt, but—and I believe this with all my heart—God wanted to teach us the type of relationship and intimacy He wanted with His creation, the only creature made in His likeness.

God does what I call divine surgery. He put Adam to sleep, pierced a hole in his side, and brought out his bride, Eve (Genesis 2:21–22).

Oh, but wait! Did I not tell you at the beginning of this book that the whole Bible was about two men, two brides, and two dilemmas? Well, hang on; it is coming.

God takes a rib from Adam and fashions Eve, Adam's helpmeet. Adam takes one look at her and says, "This is now bone of my bones And flesh of my flesh; She shall be called Woman, Because she was taken out of Man" (Genesis 2:23).

Adam was given Eve to be his bride, much like a father would give his daughter to her husband today. Adam loved his wife. Both were perfect, in a perfect environment, placed there by a perfect God.

Adam had God in him, and because Eve was taken out of Adam, she also had God in her. The life-giving Spirit that was breathed into Adam was now in his new bride, Eve.

Both were alive because the Spirit of God was in them, and He is *life*!

Apart from God, there is no life. Spiritual death is when the Spirit of God is removed from humans. Physical death is when the spirit of a human is removed from its habitat, the body.

A question I always had, and that not one pastor I ever asked had the answer for, was, "Why didn't God form Eve out of the ground when He formed Adam? Why did he take her out of Adam?" The answers varied from "For His glory" to an honest "We really don't know."

I was meditating and praying about this question one day

while imprisoned at Seagoville, Texas. I will share with you what I strongly feel the Lord placed in my heart concerning this. I am not saying He told me audibly or that I was slain by the spirit (I will explain *slain in the spirit* later) and given the answer. What I will tell you is that the answer was so clear, so vivid, and made so much sense that not only do I believe that it came from God, but I am convinced that nothing else makes sense. The Bible says that the Spirit will bear witness with the spirit (Romans 8:16), and that is what I pray will happen here.

I felt the Lord tell me that had He created Eve separate from Adam, she could not have shared in Adam's redemption; nor could anyone else born of Eve, if God had formed Adam, breathed His Spirit into him, and thus given Adam life, then separately formed Eve and given her life.

After Eve ate and instantly died spiritually and began to die physically, then her husband, Adam, followed suit, and he too ate and died. God would have had to send two redeemers: one to redeem Adam and the other to redeem Eve. But because she was taken out of Adam, when Jesus redeemed Adam, He also redeemed Eve and everyone born of Adam and Eve.

But wait—two redeemers? Let us consider that for a minute.

That also means that Jesus would have had to come down to earth twice, take on the form of men, live among men, experience everything a man experiences, yet sin not! Also, let men do to Him what they would, offer Himself as ransom on the cross, die at the hands of mortals gone amuck, be buried and rise from the dead *twice*, once for Adam and again for Eve.

But since in Adam all die, and in Christ all are made alive (1 Corinthians 15:22), He only had to do it once! Praise God!

Wow! I was blown away, and like I said, nothing else makes sense!

We can only imagine Adam's reaction the first time he saw

Eve. I can almost hear him say, "You are a man! A man with a womb, a womb-man, bone of my bone and flesh of my flesh!"

Then they were told to "Be fruitful, and multiply, and replenish the earth" (Genesis 1:28).

The use of the words *replenish the earth* tells us that earth must have been inhabited before Adam was even formed and before God restored it in Genesis 1:3–10.

The heavens were already tested. Please know that God did not want then, nor does He want now, anyone to serve Him because they must. He has always wanted us to choose to love and serve Him on our own. Like I mentioned earlier, it is one thing to stand before the throne of God and continuously say, "Holy, Holy, Holy, is the Lord God Almighty," because you have to, and quite another to say it because you want to because you love Him!

❖

CHAPTER FOUR

THE TESTING
OF ADAM

A s I have mentioned, a faith that cannot be tested is a … well, you know the rest!

As we already know, all of heaven was tested, and now God had to test His new creation. God had placed two trees in the middle of the garden—the Tree of the Knowledge of Good and Evil and the Tree of Life.

God had warned Adam that he was free to eat of any tree in the garden but not to eat of the Tree of the Knowledge of Good and Evil. He further warned him that the day he ate of it, he would surely die (Genesis 2:8, 15).

Please understand that this had nothing to do with what kind or type of fruit it was and everything to do with whether or not Adam would be obedient to God.

The Tree of Life must have produced some sort of cellular regenerating fruit that was to keep mortal humans in perpetual immortality. The tree is now in heaven according to Revelation 22:2.

God had tested the heavens, and He now had to test His new creation. Satan had a following, maybe even millions of angels that had fallen with him. I would imagine that he had power, at least as much as God would allow him to have, and I think that he could have muscled (for lack of a better word) his way into the garden, but he had no authority.

The keys, the deed to the garden, and the authority had been given to Adam, the creature created in the image of God. Satan had to come up with a plan whereby Adam would give him the deed or the authority to rule in the garden on his own.

Let me say a few words on authority that most people do not understand. There is a big difference between power and authority.

Let me give you an example. You may be a lot bigger and tougher than me. You may have the physical power to break into my house, kick me out, and try to live in it as if it was your own, but you have no authority.

I have the deed to my house, and it is in my name. I can call the cops, and they will arrest you or, at the very least, get you out. You may have the power, but I have the authority.

Satan knew that he must somehow get this man to give him the authority. He needed legal entry into the garden. Remember, Satan was the sum of intelligence when speaking of God's created creatures before Adam.

Is it any wonder that we are warned to be aware of his devices?

Lest Satan should get an advantage of us: for we are not ignorant of his devices. (2 Corinthians 2:11)

Let me remind you again that Satan means adversary, which means an enemy. He is also called the chief of the devils (Luke 11:15), the ruler of this world (John 16:11), the god of this world (2 Corinthians 4:4), and the prince of the power of the air (Ephesians 2:2).

And among other things, Satan is identified as a great dragon, a roaring lion, the vile one, the tempter, and the accuser.

Paul says, "Put on the whole armor of God, that you may be able to stand against the wiles (the schemes) of the devil" (Ephesians 6:11 NKJV).

Peter tells us in 1 Peter 5:8, "Be sober, be vigilant; because your adversary the devil walks about like a roaring lion, seeking whom he may devour" (NKJV).

I am reminded of a dream I had a few years ago. I was fighting some demons and beating them easily. I was using kicks and punches that I wish I were able to do in real life. I was using what I tell my congregation is spiritual kung fu. Suddenly, in slow motion, I saw the most beautiful lion I had ever seen, running at me. He reminded me of the lion Aslan that I saw in the movie *Narnia*.

I became paralyzed with fear. I could not move. The lion had his mouth wide open. He was roaring so loudly my soul seemed to vibrate. As soon as he was close enough, he leaped out, stretching his two front legs, and I could see his ginormous claws and razor-sharp nails ready and launching at me. Right when I thought I was dead, I heard myself yell, "In the name of Jesus!" at which point he went back on four legs and started walking away. When he was about twenty feet away, he turned around and said, "Hey, Conrad, I'll be back. That's what I do."

Beloved, Satan's greatest advantage is our ignorance of his devices. He will try anything to distract and discourage us!

Satan tries to distract us by getting our minds and our attention on material things (blue) instead of the spiritual things (red); on the gifts instead of the gift giver; on the service rather than the Savior; on the methods rather than the message; on humans rather than God (1 John 2:15–16).

We are so busy building our treasures here on earth, never

thinking that this world is but a vapor. I have performed many funeral services, and I have never seen a hearse pull a U-Haul. You can't take it with you! Jesus Himself tells us not to store treasures here on earth, because they won't last, but to store them in heaven where they will be for an eternity (Matthew 6:19–20).

Beloved, nothing reveals the heart of a person more than their wallet. Is it any wonder that Paul told his young student, "The love of money was the root of all evil" (1 Timothy 6:10)? Please note that brother Paul does not say that money is the root of all evil, but that the *love* of money is.

Oh, that we would learn to apply what Paul tells us in Colossians 3:2: "Set your affection on things above, not on things on the earth."

Jesus Himself told us in Matthew 6:33, "But seek first the kingdom of God and His righteousness, and all these things shall be added to you" (NKJV).

Satan loves nothing more than to disrupt us from serving.

He especially likes to attack after we have had a mountaintop experience—a close encounter of the God kind!

Remember in Matthew 17:1–8 when Jesus took Peter, John, and James to the mountain?

It's called the Mount of Transfiguration because Jesus was transfigured right in front of them. Jesus took three of His closest and inner circle disciples with Him to a mountain, where He proceeded to unveil Himself of His humanity and revealed to them a glimpse of His divinity.

He took off the blue suit and showed them His red reality.

None other than two of the most incredible men mentioned in the Old Testament—Moses and Elijah—showed up to discuss with Him all that He was about to experience (Luke 9:31).

Moses had been dead for about 1,500 years. Elijah had been translated and had never died but had been in paradise for about nine hundred years. Moses is a picture of the Law, and Elijah is a picture of the prophets, representing both the dead and the raptured saints.

By the way, verse 5 gives us a clear picture of the Trinity.

While he yet spake, behold, a bright cloud overshadowed them: and behold a voice out of the cloud, which said, This is my beloved Son, in whom I am well pleased; hear ye him.

The voice was the Father, Jesus the Son was standing in a radiant light, and the Holy Spirit was the overshadowing cloud.

Peter, impulsive and never missing an opportunity to speak his mind, in his lack of understanding of what was really happening, wanted to build three tabernacles: one for Jesus, one for Moses, and one for Elijah (verse 4).

Now we are not told what Peter was thinking when he suggested this. Maybe he wanted to set up camp there and never come down. Maybe he thought they were at the very least going to spend some time up there and that they needed shelter.

But we do know that, in his asking, he was in effect placing Moses and Elijah in equal standing with Jesus, something the Father was not going to permit. "While he was still speaking, behold, a bright cloud overshadowed them; and suddenly a voice came out of the cloud, saying, 'This is My beloved Son, in whom I am well pleased. Hear Him!'" (Matthew 17:5 NKJV).

In other words, the Father was telling them, "Don't *ever* compare My Son with *anyone*! Listen to Him and Him only!"

It's funny how the world loves to compare Jesus with many men. They compare Him to Mohammed, Buddha, Confucius, or Lao Tzu, even Gandhi. Yet God tells them what He said to Peter around two thousand years ago. "This is My beloved Son, In whom I am well pleased. Hear Him!"

It is as if God the Father was letting Peter and us know that only in His Son, Jesus, was He well pleased.

And it is only because we who are born again are in Christ that the Father is pleased with us.

Verse 6 then tells us that when Peter, John, and James heard the voice, they fell on their faces and were afraid. Then Jesus walked up to them, touched them, and told them not to be afraid (verse 7).

I recently did a sermon called "One Touch!" Wow. Can you imagine being physically touched by God Himself?

Jesus put on His man-suit again, walked up to them, and told them not to be afraid, then led them down the mountain. I am sure they would have preferred to stay up there. I bet they never wanted to come down.

But be ready. We must come down from the mountain, and most of the time, Satan is there waiting!

Verses 14 through 18 tell us that as soon as they walked down from the mountain, a father brought his demon-possessed son to Jesus. And that, my friend, is so typical of how Satan operates. He loves to bring us down, especially when we have just had a mountaintop experience with God.

Speaking of mountaintop experiences, let me share with you another dream I had, except this was much more than just a dream. This happened after one of the services I held with my brothers and fellow inmates at the Seagoville Correctional Institute in Seagoville, Texas. If you do not know or have not heard or watched my testimony, I did six years in both state and federal prisons for drug smuggling.

(You can watch my testimony on YouTube by searching for Pastor Conrad De La Torres, or on our website, Fusionchurch. life.)

I have to say that night was one of the most powerful nights I have ever experienced in my Christian walk. Many inmates came to Christ, lives were changed, men were transformed, and the Holy Spirit could not only be felt, but He could almost be touched!

It was lights-out time, and everyone had to be in their bunks for lockdown. I had climbed into my top bunk while my roommate was already asleep and snoring on the bottom bunk. He was a great guy and a devout Catholic, and while he put up with my constant teaching and preaching, he never attended any of our evangelical services. I asked him once what it was about the Catholic Church that attracted him so much, and his response was "The rituals."

As I lay down, I fell asleep singing praises and thanking God for what He had just done in our service. I immediately went into a dream where I found myself at the front door of my house, walking in. As I opened the door, my precious daughter, Monique, who was around eight years old at the time, met me and was standing about ten feet in front of me, welcoming me home with the most beautiful smile you could ever imagine.

I remember that in my dream, I started to cry from the joy of seeing her and being home with my family again. As I took a step forward, Monique's smile turned into a frown, and there was a fire starting behind her. This startled me so much I woke up with a gasp, terrified. I was breathing hard, and my heart was pounding. I could hear my roommate snoring, and although I was sad to find myself in prison still, I was relieved that it was only a dream. I put my hand on my chest and calmed myself down. I slowly got my breath back, closed my eyes, and immediately found myself right back where I left off in the dream.

Monique's eyes were now turning red, and she was growling, and the fire had spread in the background. Again, I woke up with a gasp and had to catch my breath. Again, I put my hand to my chest and calmed myself down to where I could close my eyes. As I did, again I found myself right back where I had left off in my dream. Monique's eyes were now completely red. Her demeanor was, for lack of a better word, like an animal or what you would think a demon would be like.

The fire had by now consumed the entire house behind her, but she did not seem to be affected by it in any way. She just stared at me with meanness and hatred that is hard to describe. Again, I woke up completely out of breath and soaked in sweat, terrified.

I did not want to close my eyes or go back to sleep in fear that I would end up back there again and even die in my sleep. I calmed myself down, caught my breath, and decided to step down very gently and quietly so as to not disturb or wake up my roommate and go the bathroom.

Our rooms were a two-man room with bunk beds, and the bathroom was in the hall. I went to the bathroom, urinated, washed my hands and face, and stood there for a few minutes in disbelief of what I had just experienced. I went back to my room, closed the door, and climbed back on my bed.

I feel the need to describe to you these beds. They were made of metal and separately attached to the wall. The top bunk, where I slept, was higher than I have ever seen any bunk bed before in my life. I had to place my foot on my roommate's bunk, grab one of the metal posts, and hoist myself up.

As I lay back down and placed a pillow over my face (a habit that I have had ever since I was a child), I closed my eyes and immediately heard someone or something whispering into my ear at a hundred miles per hour. "You're a loser. No one loves you. What do you think? Who do you think you are? God is not going to help you. We are going to get your daughter. We are going to get your son, your wife. You are never going home. You will never see them again. God isn't real. He can't help you." And on and on. I opened my eyes, and I promise before God that what I am about to share with you is the absolute truth!

And if you know me and know anything about my ministry, you know that I teach against what I call the hyper-faith movement. I call hyper-faith the give-to-get, or word-of-faith, name-it-claim-it, blab-it-grab-it, fake-it-take-it movement that has permeated the body of Christ. This doctrine misuses and abuses the gifts of God.

Having said that, let me also say that I know spiritual beings are real, not only because the Word of God says so but also because I have seen them. Some people have accused me of not believing in the gifts of the Holy Spirit. Please let me assure you that I believe in *all* of the gifts of the Spirit—when it is the Spirit of God who does them!

I opened my eyes and saw a being that must have been over ten feet tall, hunched over, with his face on mine and with nothing between us except my pillow. This creature was completely black, and I could see his eyes staring at me from the other side of my pillow. His mouth was over my ear, and the pillow seemed to make his voice echo even more as he continued to tell me that he or they were going to destroy my family, and who did I think I was, and that God was not going to help me.

My face was almost touching his. I thank God that there was a pillow between us. I tried to yell, but I could not. I was petrified!

I was saying, "In Jesus's name!" over and over but could only say it in my mind. Finally, after what seemed to be an eternity, I heard myself yell out, "In the name of Jesus!" as loudly as I could, and the creature disappeared.

My roommate was so startled that he jumped up, hit his head on the bottom of my bed, and screamed. Everyone on the entire floor was awake and out of their rooms, wondering what had happened. Needless to say, I was embarrassed and asked for forgiveness and explained it as a bad dream, afraid that I was going to be labeled a nut, although I did share it with the brothers and used it as a teaching tool.

Beloved, believe me when I tell you that the devil wants to discourage us and spiritually deflate us like a spiritual balloon. And he will use any and every means he can think of to do it.

Sometimes it is your friends and even your own family he uses. I think of Moses, one of the two men on the Mount of Transfiguration with Jesus and His disciples. My goodness, the stuff he had to put up with, all the murmuring and complaining. He was even in danger of being killed by the very people he had just led out of slavery in Egypt. Read the books of Deuteronomy and Numbers. You will be amazed, and you will see why Moses was a type of Christ.

No wonder the book of Numbers says that he was the humblest man on the face of the earth (Numbers 12:3).

Yes, Satan especially loves to use those closest to us to discourage us.

But I love and am encouraged by brother Paul, who said, "And let us not be weary in well doing: for in due season we shall reap, if we faint not" (Galatians 6:9).

So never quit!

Beloved, the devil makes you think you'll never make it! But faith says to *never, never, never, give up*! "With God all things are possible" (Matthew 19:26).

When we find ourselves in the valleys of life, we often find ourselves saying, "Eli, Eli, lama sabachthani?" (My God, my God, why has thou forsaken me?) (Matthew 27:46)

Proverbs 13:12 tells us, "Hope deferred makes the heart sick" (NKJV).

I was just reminded of this truth recently as one of our precious couples and the heads of our children's ministry were really hoping and praying that God would grant them the managerial position at a storage facility in Orlando, Florida.

They had gone to the interview with such hope and

anticipation that it broke my heart when they were told they did not get the job. Although I knew that they wanted to move from the area and were seeking employment in North Florida, we were thankful to God that they got to stay with us at least a bit longer. I felt so badly for them. I did know this though, and so did they: God knows best!

Update! A few months later, the wife was offered a position as manager at another storage company north of Ocala, Florida, and the husband was offered the supervisor's position of the company's facilities in the whole area—and a beautiful house to live in to boot! God is good!

Sometimes God allows certain things to happen in our lives that will change the direction we might be headed in. I know, looking back, that I would have never learned to rightly divide God's Word had I not gone to prison.

Please do not misunderstand. I am in no way saying that God put me in prison. On the contrary, my sin put me in prison. And if you have watched or heard my testimony, you have heard me say that I was innocent of the charges against me (bringing in cocaine with Pablo Escobar), and I was, but like the Bible says, "A man reaps what he sows" (Galatians 6:7).

I sowed a field of drugs and brought marijuana to this country and consequently reaped a field of prison. Nevertheless, God was true to His Word: "And we know that all things work together for good to those who love God, to those who are the called according to His purpose" (Romans 8:28 NKJV).

The saddest part of this is that in my utter ignorance and rebellion, I put my family through torture, and they were affected by my sin. That is something I will have to live with for the rest of my life, and I will *never* be able to redeem the years I spent away from them!

I heard many inmates wrongfully testify in the prison chapels that God had put them there, to which I would say, "Absolutely not! Your sin did." It is just that we have such a patient and merciful God who loves us so much that He will take even our very worst and, if we allow Him, guide us and see us through it, bringing us out the other side even better and stronger.

Believe me when I tell you that Satan is alive and well on planet Earth. And he has been working overtime in many people's lives.

While in prison, I spent most of my days in the Word studying. We (inmates) held our own services every day, and I can honestly tell you that some of the most mature, godly, consecrated men I have ever met were, and some still are, in prison. We learned from one another, encouraged one another, and were there for one another. We grew to trust the Lord and learned to rightly divide His Word with one another. Beloved, when God is all you have, you come to understand that God is all you need!

We were also blessed to have incredible brothers and sisters who volunteered each week to come to the prison and share with us and teach us God's Word. One brother I especially remember, love, and thank God for is Dennis Lyons. My goodness, that man taught us so much! He especially taught us to rightly handle the Word of God.

I learned to apply two colors to the scriptures: blue to speak of things *seen* and red to speak of things *unseen*.

As an example, I will color code 2 Corinthians 4:16–18 for you:

For which cause we faint not; but though our outward [blue] man perish, yet the inward [red] man is renewed day by day

For our light affliction [blue], which is but for a moment, worketh for us a far more exceeding and eternal weight of glory [red].

While we look not at the things which are seen [blue], but the things which are not seen [red]; for the things which are seen are temporal [blue]; but the things which are not seen are eternal [red].

A parable, for instance, is a blue story with a red truth. It's a story using things we can see (natural) to teach us about things we cannot see (spiritual).

When I visit a church, I often ask the congregation this question: "Do you need to be circumcised to get to heaven?" Of course, most, if not all, of the time, the response is an emphatic, "No!" to which I quickly respond, "Oh yes!" In the Old Testament, it was circumcision of the flesh (blue). In the New Testament, it is circumcision of the heart (red).

As a matter of fact, the entire Bible is blue or red.

If you place your Bible in front of you, and you start in the book of Genesis and turn the pages toward the book of Revelation, you will be going from blue to red illumination. The more pages you turn, the more red is dispensed. Blue types and shadows of the red realities God is trying to teach you.

The whole Bible can be divided into these two colors. It will help you to rightly divide the Word, and you will find that the Word will come alive as you read and understand it.

Most people take the Word of God out of context, which leads to all kinds of wrong doctrine. Therefore, brother Paul told his young son in the faith to study the Word of God so that he would be able to handle it (rightly divide it) correctly and never be ashamed (2 Timothy 2:15).

And to understand it, you must make sure that what you read is in context. You may have to read above or below the verse you read, and you may even have to read the whole chapter or book to get the full meaning or context.

So, the first question you should ask yourself when studying the Word of God is "Is it in context?" The number one problem I see in the body of Christ is that most churches or people do not handle or apply the Bible correctly. They will take a verse and make a whole doctrine out of it.

Scripture will interpret scripture. We must study the whole counsel of the Word. We need to consider not only what is written but also by whom, to whom, from where, at what time, for what purpose, to what intent, and under what circumstances, always considering what was said before and what was said after.

Back to our story ...

Satan went to the woman, Eve, and convinced her that the reason God did not want them to eat of the Tree of Life was because God knew that the day they ate, they would not need Him any longer, and they would become gods themselves.

In other words, Satan told them (to color code it), "Right now, you have red in you, but God knows that the day you eat from the tree, you will be completely red, and you won't need Him anymore."

He caused Eve to doubt the Word of God. Genesis 3:1 says, "Yea, hath God said, Ye shall not eat of every tree of the garden?"

Eve saw that the fruit was good to eat and good to make one wise and to make one like God, so she ate. And when she ate, she died!

Instantly, the Spirit of God departed from her, and she died spiritually. It was as if the light of her spirit had been snuffed out. Much like blowing out a candle!

When illustrating this with my blue and red cups, I place the red cup inside the blue one to represent the Spirit of God inside her. The second she eats, I take the red cup out, and the blue is left empty and desolate, illustrating that she is now spiritually dead and physically dying, which brings us to the dilemma.

❖

CHAPTER FIVE

THE DILEMMA
OF ADAM

The Bible tells us that Adam was right there with Eve when she ate of the fruit (Genesis 3:6).

You might have to read this verse several times to really get your head around it because it is hard to believe that Adam was right there while the serpent was seducing his wife and did not do anything about it. Adam should have grabbed that serpent by the neck and bit his head right off! At the very least, he should have demanded that the serpent leave the garden, never to return.

Adam was the one responsible not only for the garden but also for his wife, Eve. Let me take this opportunity to say something to my brothers right here. *You* are responsible for the spiritual atmosphere in your home! *You* are the one who will have to give an account for what you allowed in your home! *You* are the priest of the house! *You* are the one who needs to lead. And let me add this: it is hard for a woman to follow a man that is going nowhere!

Eve ate first, yet we will see that God came looking for Adam. He was responsible, and he had to give an account!

It's unbelievable to me that he just stood there as Eve was convinced to eat the forbidden fruit, then watched her do it. But, then again, if we were to be honest with ourselves, how often do we let things that we know go contrary to the Word of God enter our homes and our lives?

Please understand that Adam had just witnessed the spiritual death of his wife. The connection she once had with God, the Shekinah glory that once enshrined her, was no longer there. She was dead! She was spiritually separated from life itself, God, and for the first time, she was physically dying.

Adam was a living (spiritually and physically) man, looking at a dead (spiritually dead and physically dying) woman.

And this is when he experienced what I call *the dilemma!*

A dilemma is a problem offering two possibilities, neither of which is preferable. And I suggest to you that is exactly what Adam experienced in the Garden of Eden that day.

Adam must have thought to himself, *If I eat, I will die, but if I don't, God will remove her, and I will be alone again.*

Beloved, you and I will never really understand this until we are in the presence of God Himself. I can almost hear him say to the Lord, "It was You who gave her to me. I would rather never have met her than to lose her. I love her. Please don't take her from me!"

What an incredible battle he must have gone through! What a war he must have experienced between his flesh and his spirit. From this day on, every twice-born man (born of woman and God) will have to fight this battle within themselves.

We get a glimpse of this with brother Paul. He speaks of something similar he experienced roughly four thousand years later when he wrote the book of Romans. In chapter 7, he shares the battle he had with his flesh and spirit (Romans 7:18–24).

My goodness, what a dilemma! What a battle Adam must

have gone through. He found himself having to choose between God, his Creator, and his wife, Eve.

I think he looked at God, looked at Eve, looked at God, looked at Eve, looked at God, looked at Eve, and never looked up again.

And he stood there, with his eyes wide open, knowingly, willfully, and understanding that God had told them that the day they ate, they would surely die. Knowing that it would cost him his life, his position, his intimacy, and friendship with his Creator, his God, Adam ate. And when he ate, he died!

Adam chose to be separated from God rather than be separated from Eve, his bride, his wife, the woman (the only woman, may I add) he loved.

Please understand this. Adam and Eve did not just cut their lives short and so die before their time when they ate of the fruit. They introduced into their body something that was not there before, a new element—mortality.

They were created to live forever. Genesis 3:22–24 tells us that although the poison of the fruit (we will call it *syn-nesence*) had done its damage, had introduced death to the bodies of Adam and Eve, they could have eaten of the Tree of Life and reversed that damage.

The problem was that, while this tree apparently could heal mortality and thus allow them to live forever, it could have done nothing to heal or revive their dead spirit.

So God expelled them from the garden. Not because He was mad at them, as some suppose. Not to punish them. Not to teach them a lesson but because He loved them. He moved them out of the garden so they could not eat of the Tree of Life and live forever spiritually dead and separated from God. God, in His love, went as far as to place an angel and a flaming sword to guard the tree (Genesis 3:22–24).

Because of the fall of man, God had to break His rest (Genesis 2:2) and went looking for the man.

❖

CHAPTER SIX

WHERE ARE YOU?

A dam and Eve heard the Lord God walking in the cool of the
day in the garden, and they hid themselves. Hid themselves
from the God that had created them. Hid themselves from
the Creator that had given them life and sustained them. Hid
themselves because, for the first time since their creation, they
saw their nakedness and were ashamed (Genesis 3:8–10).

And that has been the condition of every son of Adam and
daughter of Eve ever since: naked, ashamed, and trying to cover
ourselves with any and every fig leaf we can find.

Sin separated God from Adam and Eve just as it separates us
today, and we have been trying to hide from God ever since. If
we would only understand that it is impossible to hide from God!
Nothing is hidden from Him.

Where can I go from Your Spirit? Or where can I flee from
Your presence? (Psalm 139:7 NKJV)

When God came to them in the garden, He asked Adam,
"Where are you?" (NKJV). Please do not think for a moment

that God did not know where he was. God knew exactly where he was. He knew for sure that Adam was not where He had left Him. It was as if that invisible, spiritual, red umbilical cord that connected Adam to God had been severed.

He knew where he was. He just wanted Adam to know it. And I believe that from that time until now, God has asked every son of Adam and daughter of Eve that very same question: "Where are you?"

He wants us to come from behind our trees and allow Him to openly deal with us. You and I are masters at hiding behind trees to cover our true spiritual condition.

When I was younger, I hid behind a lot of mango trees, but my father would always catch me stealing mangos and whoop my behind.

One of the trees we love to hide behind is the Tree of False Feelings. Yet the Bible plainly teaches us that we should "walk by faith, not sight" (2 Corinthians 5:7).

Feelings, unless they are lined up with the truth of God's Word, can be treacherous and lead us into wrong and crazy doctrines.

Many people, based on nothing more than blue feelings and emotions, have gone to the altar, have been moved, have cried, and some said that they have even been slain in the spirit.

By the way, there is only one instance in the whole New Testament where you can find a true slain in the Spirit, and that is in the case of Ananias and Sapphira (Acts 5:1–11).

This word of faith false doctrine, which should really be called the walk by feelings movement, has done more harm and has led more people away from truth and into false teachings and doctrine than anything else in the body of Christ!

People think they are operating under the influence of the spirit, and they are, but it is *not* the Spirit of God. It is nothing more than faith on faith—faith in what they are feeling at the time, not faith in what God has to say in His Word.

Now the Spirit speaketh expressly, that in the latter times some shall depart from the faith, giving heed to seducing spirits, and doctrines of devils. (1 Timothy 4:1)

This has led many to be misled by anyone who professes to be a prophet! I call them prophaliars.

Paul warns us in Ephesians 4:14, "That we henceforth be no more children, tossed to and fro, and carried about with every wind of doctrine, by the sleight of men, and cunning craftiness, whereby they lie in wait to deceive."

And there are many other trees we hide behind: the trees of religion, lying, stealing, adultery, addiction, fornication, fear, failure, unbelief, idolatry, unforgiveness, immorality, and the list goes on and on!

Back to Genesis 3.

Adam told God that he was hiding because he was naked. "Who told you that you were naked?" God asked him (Genesis 3:11). And here, beloved, we have the first snitch that ever lived! The man pointed (I think) to his wife and told God, "The woman *you* gave me!"

I have always wondered what God would have done had Adam owned up to his mistake and taken full responsibility for what happened. I guess we can speculate all we want on this, but we won't know until we meet the Lord.

Eve looked around, and maybe she said to Adam, "Oh no, you just didn't!" and pointed at the snake (I think) and told God, "The snake deceived me" (Genesis 3:13).

And things just went downhill from there. The snake looked around, but all the other animals had run away. (Not really, I just made that up.) We do know that God cursed the snake, the man, the woman, the ground, everything!

And in verse 15, we have the first mention of Jesus the Christ in the Bible.

And I will put enmity Between you and the woman, And between your seed and her Seed; He shall bruise your head, And you shall bruise His heel. (NKJV)

The words *her seed* are speaking about none other than Jesus Himself! And the words "He shall bruise your head, and you shall bruise His heel" are saying that while Satan may ultimately put Jesus to death on a cross (bruise His heel), that very act will be the thing that will kill him (bruise your head). How interesting that the Holy Spirit would use those two words to tell us about what was going to happen. Bruise the *heel* of Jesus and bruise the *head* of Satan. *Heel* speaks of a wound that one can recover from (resurrection), while *head* speaks of fatality, a wound from which you will not recover!

❖

CHAPTER SEVEN

BLUE PEOPLE HAVE BLUE BABIES

B y blue, I mean that two spiritually dead people have spiritually dead babies. Death entered humanity through the man Adam and is passed to all humans through his seed.

Therefore, just as through one man sin entered the world, and death through sin, and thus death spread to all men, because all sinned. (Romans 5:12 NKJV)

Adam's descendants were born in his likeness, for we read in Genesis 5:3 that Adam "begat a son in his own likeness, and after his image." In other words, spiritually dead, separated from a living God.

That is why I say two mortal, natural, earthly, blue (take your pick) people procreate blue babies. All men born of men are sons of men until they are born again (John 3:3–7) and become sons of God.

So God looks down from heaven to mortals made in His likeness after the Fall (when Adam ate) and says, "For all have sinned and fall short of the glory of God" (Romans 3:23 NKJV), and in Romans 3:10, He says, "As it is written: 'There is none righteous, no, not one'" (NKJV).

I will color code these verses for you. There are none red filled—not one! There are none who have red in them, for all are sinners and blue!

You and I, my beloved, were born spiritually dead! We were born with the poison of Adam running through our mortal bodies. Death was conceived in Adam and birthed the moment Adam sinned. We just read the scripture that says, "By one man (Adam) sin entered into the world and death by sin" (Romans 5:12).

The father of death is sin, and his grandfather is Satan. So on the day that Adam fell to temptation and sinned, there was a bouncing baby boy born into the household of the devil by the name of *death*!

No wonder the Bible tells us in 1 John 3:8 that "He who sins is of the devil, for the devil has sinned from the beginning. For this purpose, the Son of God was manifested, that He might destroy the works of the devil" (NKJV).

Please understand that before death was born, the world was perfect. There were no thorns, no thistles, no rust, no pain, no labor. The fruit of the land yielded itself willingly.

The human body was made perfect and was created to last for an eternity in fellowship with its Creator God. We are the only creature made in His likeness in that we are a trichotomy. We are a triune being. We are body, soul, and spirit.

Before the Fall, our spirit was alive and connected (if you will) to the Spirit of God. But death changed all that. The human body began to decay and deteriorate. Adam's body started to decay the instant he ate of the forbidden fruit. It took physical death 930 years to run its course through the body of Adam.

Death rapidly became the strongest predator on the face of

the earth. It does not take us long at all to see him surface in Cain, who strikes down his own brother, Abel, in a field and leaves him there to have his blood swallowed by the earth.

Death plays no favorites and is not prejudiced. He attacks young, old, man, woman, and child alike. He does not care about race, nationality, language, position, or status. He walks to and fro on the earth, seeking whom he may devour.

Of the millions of men and women who have ever lived on this earth, only two have escaped his clutches: Enoch (Genesis 5:24) and Elijah (2 Kings 2:11).

Please know that there is a difference between the *syn* we inherited from Adam and the *sins* we commit.

We spell it syn because it is through the Y chromosome of Adam that we receive it. The reason we sin is because we have the poison of syn in us. We call it syn-nesence! In other words, our behavioral sins are because of our positional syn.

We are not *synners* because we sin. We sin because we are synners! And since we all come from Adam, we are all born spiritually dead, physically dying, and with the poison of syn running through our mortal bodies.

It is for this reason that we cannot work enough, buy enough, be good enough or religious enough, or do anything that will cause a perfect, holy, righteous God to allow an imperfect, spiritually dead, physically dying, and decaying man or woman to enter His perfect kingdom, much less enter His perfect presence!

❖

CHAPTER EIGHT

THE SECOND MAN ... GOD WITH US

R omans 6:23 says, "For the wages of sin is death, but the gift of God is eternal life in Christ Jesus our Lord" (NKJV).

Now I know that I shared this verse a bit earlier, but I want you to especially notice the second half of the verse: "but the gift of God is eternal life in Christ Jesus our Lord."

God had declared that Adam's sin brought death to all of humanity. Remember, "There are none righteous, no, not one." (Romans 3:10)

So someone had to pay the penalty demanded by the Father, which was death. Adam could not pay it; Adam was dead. It needed to be someone with life, both physically and spiritually, and not one was found on earth.

The best Adam (or any of us, for that matter) could have offered was the rest of his life. Because he was spiritually dead and physically dying, he had an appointment with death. It might have taken him 930 years to die, but die he did. "And as it is appointed for men to die once, but after this the judgment" (Hebrews 9:27 NKJV).

But—there's that beautiful word again—then God stepped in. Around four thousand years later, God handpicked a young lady, a blue lady, by the name of Mary. I pray that by now you understand the color system. Again, by blue I mean spiritually dead and physically dying. I suggest to you that Mary, like David of old, had a heart after God's heart.

We find a beautiful account of this in Luke 1:26–38.

But I want to focus on verse 38: "Then Mary said, 'Behold the maidservant of the Lord! Let it be to me according to your word.' And the angel departed from her" (NKJV).

At the very instant that Mary said, "Let it be to me according to your word," the Spirit of the Living God impregnated her with His seed—the seed of God, fulfilling the prophecy God had told the serpent in the Garden of Eden concerning the seed of Eve (Genesis 3:15).

And nine months later, Mary gave birth to God in the flesh!

"Behold, the virgin shall be with child, and bear a Son, and they shall call His name Immanuel," which is translated, "God with us." (Matthew 1:23 NKJV)

Mary indeed had a little lamb—and His name was Jesus!

Mary went and visited her cousin Elizabeth in the hill country of Judah. The angel Gabriel had told Mary that her cousin was also going to have a baby in her old age and that, in fact, Elizabeth was already six months' pregnant.

Please know that the baby boy that Elizabeth was carrying was none other than John the Baptist, who the prophet Isaiah had said was going to be a voice in the wilderness and prepare the way for Christ (Isaiah 40:3).

But right now, I want to focus on something just awesome!

Let's read verse 44 of Luke chapter 1. Now please know that this is when Mary first sees her cousin Elizabeth: "For indeed, as soon as the voice of your greeting sounded in my ears, *the babe leaped in my womb for joy!*" (NKJV) (emphasis mine).

Did you see it? Did you notice something incredible? Something awesome? Something that was the first to ever happen?

Read verse 44 again: "For indeed, as soon as the voice of your greeting sounded in my ears, *the babe leaped in my womb for joy*" (Again, emphasis mine).

That, beloved, is the first mention of the worship of Jesus as a human in the Bible—intra-uterus worship!

Incredible!

Mary goes on to sing and praise her God. Read it, beloved. It is beautiful. Mary could sing and praise because she already knew what God was about to do—save us!

But I wonder if she ever realized that the little baby boy she was going to have was older than her and the same age as His Father. That God would single her out to carry the eternal Word in her womb, and that through her, the Word was to become flesh. Emmanuel, God with us, God one of us, is too much to take in now. I can only imagine what she must have thought and felt. My goodness!

And do you want to know something incredible? God has also handpicked you and me for that very same purpose. Our bodies were each specially created to be a dwelling place for God.

Well, that little baby turned out to be the last Adam of 1 Corinthians 15:45–49. The book of Ruth speaks of Him as the Kinsman Redeemer. Jesus is the *only* person who could have ever redeemed Adam, for there was never another Adam on earth until Jesus!

It had to be a kinsman, a family member. And at the Fall, the pure Adamite (man alive with the Spirit of God in him) as God created him became extinct on earth; there were no Adams found. No kinsman redeemer. So God had to become an Adam so that He might redeem Adam.

There have only been two red-filled men who ever walked

this earth—the first and the last Adams. So when the first Adam died and needed redemption, only the second and last Adam could have redeemed him. When the first Adam lost his red, there was no other human who had any red to give him. So a red God from heaven had to take the form of a blue man from earth and pay for the mistake the first red-filled man made, so that He could offer red to any blue person who would receive it.

Pretty simple, huh? I think so!

Who is like unto the LORD our God, who dwelleth on high, Who humbleth himself to behold the things that are in heaven, and in the earth! (Psalm 113:5–6)

Great is the LORD, and greatly to be praised; and his greatness is unsearchable. (Psalm 145:3)

But then again, how could I even be expected to explain such a being? How can I describe the indescribable?

This is why the sin of idolatry is such an abomination to God. This is why He told Moses in Exodus 20:4, "You shall not make for yourself a carved image—any likeness of anything that is in heaven above, or that is in the earth beneath, or that is in the water under the earth" (NKJV).

Think about it. What measurements would you use? How would you—how could you—measure the immeasurable? You might as well try to put a Tupperware lid over the Grand Canyon.

Beloved, life's hidden hunger is Jesus, and some are too blind to see it. He is the great need of the human heart. The creation itself groans for Him (Romans 8:18, 19, 22, 23)!

There is a song that goes something like this: "My hope is built on nothing less than Jesus Christ and righteousness!"

And our hope is God, who robed Himself in human flesh and became Immanuel ("God with us") in the person of the Lord Jesus Christ! Down from a kingdom to a cross, from majesty to misery, from a throne to a tree.

Are you understanding this?

The one who created everything that has ever been created (John 1:3; Colossians 1:16) and in whom *all things consist* (Colossians 1:17) is now dependent upon the very creature He created!

The book of Hebrews puts it this way:

Who being the brightness of His glory and the express image of His person, and upholding all things by the word of His power, when He had by Himself purged our sins, sat down at the right hand of the Majesty on high. (Hebrews 1:3 NKJV)

There were many children at that time named Jesus. But there was only one who could be called *Emmanuel*!

"For a child will be born to us" (He was born in a stable in Bethlehem). "A son will be given to us" (He was given at the cross) (Isaiah. 9:6).

If Adam just needed information, God would have sent him a teacher. But he needed a Redeemer, so God came Himself.

❖

CHAPTER NINE

TWO GARDENS

Remember I told you that the Bible condensed is the story of two (the first and the last) Adams, two gardens (Eden and Gethsemane), and two ... well, I will tell you more later.

Matthew gives us a detailed account of the last night Jesus spent with His disciples. He had instructed them as to what to do and where they were going to partake of the Passover meal, or what is often referred to as the Last Supper (Mathew 26:17–19).

As you may know, Passover (Pesah or Pesach in Hebrew) is a Jewish holiday commemorating when the Hebrews were liberated from slavery in Egypt. The Lord was going to send one last plague on Egypt, and this one was going to include the Jews as well.

The Lord had instructed Moses to tell the people of Israel what to do to survive the plague. Each household was to take a one-year-old male lamb without blemish, tend to it for four days, then at twilight on the fourteenth day of that month, kill the lamb, take some of the blood, and put it on the two sides of the door of the house and on the top.

He further instructed them to roast the lamb and eat it with unleavened bread and bitter herbs. None of it should remain, but if some did, they were to burn it. They were also instructed to eat it quickly, dressed and ready to go.

The Lord was going to pass through the land of Egypt that night, on both beast and man. If when He passed, He did not see the blood of the lamb on the doorpost, He would kill the firstborn of the family inside. If He saw the blood, He would pass over and spare the family (Exodus12:1–14).

What a beautiful picture of God seeing the blood of His Lamb (Jesus) on the doorposts of our hearts, passing by and sparing us from death (John 1:29)!

We can only imagine what was going through Jesus's mind as He sat there having this last meal with His chosen disciples, knowing that none of them really understood, that one of them would deny that he even knew Him—three times at that—and that one of them was going to betray and sell Him as one sells cattle. And not only that, but he knew what was about to happen to Him in just a few hours, not to mention the kind of death that awaited Him.

Beloved, it is hard to believe that He even made it to the garden. You would think that He would have given up the ghost just by that.

In one last attempt to teach them and tell them what was going to happen, He took the bread and blessed it. He told them that the bread was His body, which would be broken for them. I wish I had the power to go back and just look at their faces when Jesus was telling them that. I wonder if they could tell what He was going through. I wonder if they knew that He was so sad because He knew that He was going to die. I wonder if He was shaking through all of that. I wonder!

After they had eaten, he took the cup, blessed it, and told them that the cup was the cup of the New Testament, His blood that would be shed for their sins and the sins of the world. That every time they partook of that meal, every time they ate that bread and drank that cup, they would remember Him until He comes back (1 Corinthians 11:23–26).

He then looked at His betrayer, Judas, and told him, "What you are about to do, do quickly" (John 13:27). And they departed to Gethsemane.

It is by no coincidence that Jesus went to the Garden of Gethsemane on the Mount of Olives. Gethsemane means oil press.

I think it was Alexander the Great, when looking over the Valley of Megiddo, who said it was the greatest battlefield he had ever seen. And we know that the battle of Armageddon will be fought there, but, beloved, believe me when I tell you that the two greatest battles of history were fought in gardens.

As I thought of the first Adam in the first garden, I noticed something I had never noticed before. I noticed that the Bible never says that Adam was lonely but that God said it was not good for him to be alone.

God was, in essence, saying, for us to understand Him, we must understand relationships, and we cannot understand relationships unless we have someone to relate to.

God reached in and took a part of Adam to make Eve, the sum of His earthly creation that was to bring new ones into the world.

The Garden of Eden was the place of humanity's first battle. And there Adam saw something so beautiful and special in Eve that he chose her over his own life! He did not resist temptation and chose his will over the Father's will.

In the Garden of Gethsemane, the second Adam, Jesus Christ, saw something so beautiful and special in us that He chose us over His own death. He chose the Father's will over His own (human) will.

Beloved, the pain, the war, was at the cross, but the battle was fought in the garden.

Just as Adam's decision in Eden affected all who are related to Adam in death, so Christ's decision in Gethsemane affects all who are related to Him in life. You could not get a clearer picture of love submitted than the Garden of Gethsemane!

The Sunday before, as He entered Jerusalem riding on a colt, thousands were singing, "Hosanna! Blessed is the King of Israel that cometh in the name of the Lord!" And Jesus accepted their praises, knowing that before the end of the week, these same people would be asking for His death.

On Monday, Jesus, filled with righteous indignation, entered the temple and confronted those who had turned His Father's house into a place of business. With a handmade whip, He drove out the merchants and overturned the tables (Matthew 21:12).

On Tuesday, as He was giving the people some final glimpses of the kingdom of God before His suffering, His enemies approached. "Who do you think you are? By what authority are you doing these things?" The people who should have known, who by years of study should have recognized and welcomed Him, sought to trap Him. And before the week was over, they would cast their votes to have Him put to death.

On Wednesday, one of His close friends who had walked with Him for three years and got to know His very heart betrayed Him and sold Him like cattle to His enemies. Not because of some ideological difference. Not because he saw or heard our Lord do or say something wrong. Not even Christ's enemies could do that. "Then said Pilate to the chief priests and to the people, I find no fault in this man" (Luke 23:4). "And they were astonished at his doctrine: for he taught them as one that had authority, and not as the scribes" (Mark 1:22). No, this betrayal was for money—for thirty pieces of silver, the price of a common slave.

On Thursday night, Jesus had one final meal with His disciples. He had one last night, one last time to try to teach His followers, His friends. One last night to prepare them for what was coming. He knew they were weak. He knew all of them would scatter. He knew Peter, His closest friend, would deny three times that he even knew Him.

He watched as Judas left the table and knew that in a few hours, he would return with soldiers to have Him arrested. He knew that in spite of all his efforts, His disciples didn't understand the significance of this night.

He knew that though they were with Him bodily, He was very much alone. And in this utter loneliness, with a heart that was about to explode from sorrow, Jesus entered the Garden of Gethsemane.

❖

CHAPTER TEN

THE DILEMMA OF
THE LAST ADAM

Oh, my goodness! I pray that as you read this part, the Holy Spirit enables you to grasp, if even just a little, the seriousness, the sacredness, the importance, the pain, and especially the dilemma, both spiritually and physically, our Lord experienced as He battled the greatest battle ever fought on planet Earth.

Then He said to them, *"My soul is exceedingly sorrowful, even to death. Stay here and watch with Me."* (Matthew 26:38 NKJV) (emphasis mine)

I remember this verse going through my mind the day I was pronounced guilty. I had turned down several offers from the district attorney in Miami, the last being four years in the old guidelines, whereby I would have had to serve maybe two. Please keep in mind that I was facing (according to them) 250 years in prison.

Never for a second did I think that God would allow me to be separated from my family for something I did not do. I had already served five years' probation for smuggling marijuana into this country. I had already repented and consecrated my life to Him. I had already started Warriors for Christ Ministries in Franklin, North Carolina. I was starting to get speaking engagements to preach.

So *never* did the thought cross my mind that my God, my Savior, my Friend, and Shepherd, would allow me to be found guilty of something of which I was innocent. I had never brought in cocaine with Pablo Escobar.

When I heard the word *guilty*, my heart almost stopped. I felt my soul trying to leave my body. This is not a metaphor or an "it felt like" or "it was almost as if." No, my soul tried to leave my body. I almost died standing up!

In an instant, several things went through my mind. The first of which was, and I told God this, "You are a lie! You are not real! I have wasted all these years!"

(Watch my testimony, and you will get the whole story. Maybe I will write another book about that someday.)

I was numb. I did not want to turn around and look at my wife or my father and mother, who were there that day.

Another thing that went through my mind was that I was going to commit suicide, that there was no way I was going to live without my wife and children.

Then the words that Jesus told His disciples in the garden went through my mind. "My soul is exceedingly sorrowful, even to death." And I asked the Lord, whom I had just renounced, "Am I tapping into what Jesus went through in the garden? Is this what He felt like? Am I tapping into that?"

I turned around, looked at Patty, my wife, who was as numb as I was, and lifted my index finger to heaven as if to say, "He's in control." But I can tell you now that at that moment, it wasn't faith; it was instinct! I wanted to somehow encourage Patty.

But enough of that. Let's continue where we left off.

Matthew 26:39 gives us a glimpse into His incredible dilemma:

And he went a little farther, and fell on his face, and prayed, saying, O my Father, if it be possible, let this cup pass from me: nevertheless not as I will, but as thou wilt.

O my Father, if it be possible, let this cup pass from me. Wow! Every time I say this verse or read it, I can hear Ted Neeley, the man who played Jesus in the 1973 musical *Jesus Christ Superstar*, sing those words to the Father in the Garden of Gethsemane. Wow!

Jesus was so hurt, prayed so hard, and was going through such pain and anguish that Luke 22:44 says His sweat became like drops of blood. How deep the darkness must have been for Jesus that night as He fought the final battle between His humanity and His deity, between the blue and the red.

Have you ever seen a greater demonstration of both the weakness of the flesh and the love of God combined?

He went away again the second time, and prayed, saying, O my Father, if this cup may not pass away from me, except I drink it, thy will be done. (Matthew 26:42)

He was, in essence, asking His Father if there was any "other way that they (humans) can be united to us, one with us, saved, redeemed, without me having to die? If not my Father, Your will, not mine be done!"

Judas, who had walked with Jesus for three years and had seen all that the other disciples had seen, but whose heart was far from God, walked up to God and betrayed Him with a kiss! Peter, James, and John were there but were oblivious to the battle.

Like the first Adam, the last Adam found Himself in an incredible dilemma. *If I eat, I die. If I don't eat, I will abide alone!*

So, He looked at us, looked at God, and asked, "Father is there any other way Conrad (put your name here) can be with us, if I don't drink of this bitter cup?" Then He looked at God and said, "But not my will, but yours be done!" (Luke 22:42 NKJV).

Like I said—two gardens, two dilemmas, two brides, two decisions.

In Gethsemane's garden, we see the greatest test of that challenge hurled at Jesus upon the cross. "Are you not the Christ? Save yourself and us!"

And therein lies the agony of that night. He could not save others and Himself. That was impossible! Here in this oil press of the garden's shadow, the culmination of all He was to suffer took place, and the reality of the cross finally took shape.

Yet He knelt and prayed, "Not my will but Thine be done," His heart broken for a broken creation, for a creature gone crazy, for humanity gone wild.

Gethsemane's battle was the start of three days that would shake the foundations of heaven and earth in the shadows of the cross.

And so, He gave His life over to mortals to do whatever they wanted! And they dragged Him in front of the chief priests, the captains of the temple, and the elders—all blinded by their religion.

Their eyes were so blind that instead of seeing the Christ, they saw a criminal; instead of seeing a teacher, they saw a traitor; instead of seeing a priest, they saw a perpetrator, a blasphemer. So blinded by their rules and religion that they rejected the very one who had come to save them. So blinded in their hearts that they completely missed all that they had been so diligently searching for. They who searched and waited and searched and waited missed their day of visitation!

And shall lay thee even with the ground, and thy children within thee; and they shall not leave in thee one stone upon another; because thou knewest not the time of thy visitation. (Luke 19:44)

They missed Him, the fulfillment of all their religious searching and the answer to all their prayers. Then after they mocked, beat, punched, and had their fun, they crowned the King of kings with a crown made of thorns and led Him to the Romans, who beat Him half to death and led Him to the cross.

❖

CHAPTER ELEVEN

THE CROSS

In the first garden (Eden), the first Adam died for his bride, Eve. In the second garden (Gethsemane), the second Adam died for His bride, the church.

God took the first Adam, put Him to sleep on the ground, pierced a hole in his side, and brought out his bride, Eve. Four thousand years later, God took the second Adam (Jesus), put Him to sleep on a cross, pierced His side, and brought out His bride, the church!

And they crucified Him.

And about the ninth hour Jesus cried out with a loud voice, saying, Eli, Eli, lama sabachthani? that is to say, My God, My God, why hast thou forsaken Me? (Matthew 27:46)

God forsaken by God. A Crucifixion within a Crucifixion. Who can understand that?

Here is God, the Creator of the universe, suspended somewhere between heaven and earth with no home in either, carrying on Himself the sin of the whole world. Here the sinless one found Himself utterly alone for the first time in eternity.

Forsaken by both men and God!

And about the ninth hour Jesus cried with a loud voice, saying, Eli, Eli, lama sabachthani? that is to say, My God, my God, why hast thou forsaken me? (Matthew 27:46)

Let me repeat it again in case you missed it: God forsaken by God! For the first time in eternity, the Word (Jesus) was separated from the Father!

God the Father turned His back. In His holiness, He could not bear to see the syn of Adam and the sin of the world on His Son.

And when He did, it got dark on earth! "Now from the sixth hour there was darkness over all the land unto the ninth hour" (Matthew 27:45).

Beloved, believe me when I tell you that when God turns His face away from earth, it gets dark!

I tend to think that He may have also turned down the lights on earth out of His love for Mary. So that she, who had been entrusted by Him to raise His only Son, would not see the full scope of what men had done and were doing to her son.

And when Jesus had cried out with a loud voice, He said, "Father, into Your hands I commit My spirit." (Luke 23:46)

Into the hands of the God who had just forsaken Him. Into the hands that held His hands from eternity past until this day. Into the hands of the one who just days before was heard to say, "This is My Son, in whom I am well pleased." Into those hands, He commended His spirit.

And, beloved, it is into those hands we must commend our lives too!

These are the last words of Jesus, according to Luke. And then He died.

On that first Christmas, God did not place His gift under the tree. He hung Him on the tree!

He was then buried in the borrowed tomb of Joseph of Arimathea (Luke 23:50–53).

When Jesus cried, "It is finished," Satan heard the foundations under his kingdom begin to crack. Three days later, when Jesus rose from the dead, Satan witnessed the destruction of every one of his plans and schemes. He saw his power broken and himself judged. He was defeated forever by the Lord Jesus!

And Colossians 2:15 says, "And having spoiled principalities and powers, he made a show of them openly triumphing over them in it."

On that day, God gave humanity the only way, the only truth, and the only life—Jesus Christ.

He was buried. But, beloved, "Weeping may endure for a night, But joy comes in the morning" (Psalm 30:5 NKJV).

CHAPTER TWELVE

❖

HE'S ALIVE!

"Now on the first day of the week" (Luke 24:1 NKJV). This was the day that the kingdom of death was repossessed. Adam and everyone born of Adam were redeemed! This was the day death died and hell was vanquished!

But they found the stone rolled away from the tomb. (Luke 24:2 NKJV)

Not to let Jesus out but to let us in!

He is not here but is risen! (Luke 24:6 NKJV)

And therein, beloved, lies our hope! There were many men crucified in the time of Jesus. There might have even been some by the name of Jesus! But *only one* rose from the dead. *Only one* was sinless. *Only one* was and is the Christ! Emanuel, God with us.

In Revelation 1:18, Jesus Himself said, "I am he that liveth and was dead; and, behold, I am alive for evermore … and have the keys of hell and death."

God sent an angelic messenger with the good news that Jesus was alive from the dead (Matthew 28:3–7). Never has the world heard a message like that one! It still reverberates through the halls of time and will throughout eternity. He is alive!

❖

CHAPTER THIRTEEN

IT'S FREE

————————————————

For us, two thousand years removed from the resurrection, the message has not changed. We still need to hear the good news that Jesus has risen from the dead. He is alive today, and there is hope for tomorrow!

Wherefore he is able also to save them to the uttermost that come unto God by him, seeing he ever liveth to make intercession for them. (Hebrews 7:25)

But God commendeth his love toward us, in that, while we were yet sinners, Christ died for us. (Romans 5:8)

Who is Jesus to you? It is a question that must be faced by every person.

Jesus posed it to His disciples, "Whom say ye that I am?" (Matthew 16:15)

Peter had the right answer. Do you?

Another question that needs to be asked and answered is the one asked by Pilate in Matthew 27:22: "What shall I do then with Jesus who is called Christ?"

What is your answer to these important questions today?

One of these days, the grave will have to give up the body

that has been placed there, and that body will be forever changed into one just like that worn by our Savior, the Lord Jesus Christ. A purple (I will explain later) body that will be raised from the dead, glorified, and taken to heaven.

Beloved, the birth, life, death, and resurrection of Jesus means little or nothing if He has not been born in our hearts!

He died that we may live. He came down that we may go up. God came to be with humans that humans may go and be with God. As a matter of fact, He is right now preparing a room for us in His Father's house, and He will soon come to take us there (John 14:2).

Have you received Him?

I am not asking if you believe in Him. The demons believe, and they tremble (James 2:19).

Have you *received* Him? "But as many as received him, to them gave he power to become the sons of God, even to them that believe on his name" (John 1:12).

The Bible says in Romans 10:9–10, "That if thou shalt confess with thy mouth the Lord Jesus, and shalt believe in thine heart that God hath raised him from the dead, thou shalt be saved. For with the heart man believeth unto righteousness; and with the mouth confession is made unto salvation."

Beloved, right now, if you so choose to, you can *know* you have *eternal life* with Christ!

Say this prayer and mean it not only with your mouth but also with your heart. Because not everyone who *professes* Christ *possesses* Christ!

"Father, I am a sinner. I confess with my mouth that Jesus, Your Son, is God. He became a man, walked with men, was crucified, buried, and I believe in my heart that three days later, He rose from the dead and is seated at Your right hand. And right now, I want to receive Him as my Savior and want to make Him

Lord of my life. Thank You for giving Your life for me. In Jesus's name Amen!"

If you did that and you really meant it, you are a new creature (2 Corinthians 5:17).

And now, you, like brother Paul, can say, "O death, where is thy sting? O grave, where is thy victory? The sting of death is sin; and the strength of sin is the law. But thanks be to God, which giveth us the victory through our Lord Jesus Christ" (1 Corinthians 15:55–57).

❖

CHAPTER FOURTEEN

BAPTISM (BLUE AND RED)

N ow before I get into baptism, I am going to ask you to bear with me and let me reiterate a few things I have already touched on. I think they are that important!

I pray that after reading this book, you have a better understanding of what really happened in both gardens, the Garden of Gethsemane and the Garden of Eden, and the dilemma of the Adams.

The war might have been won at the cross, but the battle was fought in the garden. Remember that Jesus was 100 percent God and 100 percent man. He left His glory in heaven, submitted Himself to the Father, and took the form of a man. Jesus came to do the will of the Father (John 6:38).

Then Jesus answered and said to them, "Most assuredly, I say to you, the Son can do nothing of Himself, but what He sees the Father do; for whatever He does, the Son also does in like manner." (John 5:19 NKJV)

Could there be a clearer verse that tells us that He and the Father are *one*?

Please remember that Jesus was synless. Therefore, He did not sin! He could have but did not. He could have chosen to do something other than what the Father had asked of Him.

For example, if the Father had said to Him, "Son, I want you to go to Capernaum today," if He had said, "Not today, Father. I'll go some other time," that alone would have disqualified Him! That is why I say the life He lived qualified Him to die the death He died.

Remember in the Garden of Eden, Adam and Eve were perfect. They chose to sin and introduced what I call syn-nesence, the poison of sin (mortality), into the human race.

That is why Jesus could not have been born from the seed of Adam. Adam's seed was poisoned, and it is through Adam's seed the poison is passed. Yet Jesus had to be all man (or mortal). That is why God chose a mortal by the name of Mary. He also had to be all God (the only being that not only *is life* but could offer that *life*!) to redeem man.

If you only knew how long it has taken me to write this. Because even as I write this, I pray that God gives me the wisdom, and especially the gift, to be able to put down on paper what He has given me in my heart. And to let me write it in a way that anyone who reads it may not only understand it but receive it— and thus receive life.

Please remember that this has *nothing* to do with the forgiveness of our *sin* and *everything* to do with the forgiveness and redemption of Adam's *syn*.

The reason we sin is because we have syn running through our mortal bodies. For us, it is not really a matter of sin; it is a matter of life and death!

If Jesus could have just forgiven our sins and saved us, He would have never had to die.

He was forgiving sin while He was on earth (Luke 7:44–48).

Now the question you should be asking is, why did He have to die?

Why not just declare all sons of Adam and daughters of Eve forgiven? Again, because it has to do with life and death.

The Father had set a payment for the syn of Adam, and somebody had to pay it, and the payment of that syn was death (Romans 6:23a).

And because of that, Romans also tells us, "Therefore, just as through one man sin entered the world, and death through sin, and thus death spread to all men, because all sinned" (Romans 5:12 NKJV).

God left His glory (Philippians 2:6–12), became a man, walked among men, was tempted in every way a man is tempted, yet sinned not (Hebrews 4:15).

The Creator walking around His creation, dressed like one of them, taking on their form, was the only one who had the power to pay the ransom the Father had demanded for the redemption of Adam and, through that redemption, save the whole world.

I will say it yet again. Jesus was the only one who had a *life* to give.

Now, let's talk about baptism.

Jesus goes to His cousin John to be baptized. John was the last of the Old Testament prophets, handpicked by God Himself to be the forerunner and prepare the way for the Christ (Matthew 3:1–3).

In Matthew 3:11, we read that John was telling those he was baptizing, "I indeed baptize you with water unto repentance, but he that cometh after me is mightier than I, whose shoes I am not worthy to bear: he shall baptize you with the Holy Ghost, and with fire."

To color code this for you, John was saying, "I baptize you in (blue) water, but somebody mightier than me will baptize you with His Holy Spirit in the (red)."

And right in the middle of John's sermon on repentance, Jesus appeared and insisted on being baptized. We would naturally ask, "Why? Why is Jesus baptized?" Hebrews 4:15 points out that even though He was tempted in every way, "He was without sin."

So why was He baptized? He was baptized for our sin (Isaiah 53.6). "All we like sheep have gone astray; we have turned, everyone, to his own way; and the LORD has laid on Him the iniquity of us all" (Isaiah 53:6 NKJV).

Jesus wanted to be baptized, but John tried to talk Him out of it. He knew Jesus did not need to be baptized as per forgiveness of sin. He had none (Matthew 3:13–17).

It is as if Jesus was showing John that Jesus needed to be baptized by John so that He might be identified with men. "But there is a day coming when I will baptize men so that men may identify with Me!"

(I just yelled, "Glory!")

I feel led to explain baptism a little better here, because there are a lot of misconceptions, wrong teachings, and wrong doctrines concerning baptism.

As a matter of fact, there are even false sects and denominations that teach (falsely) that you cannot be saved unless you are water baptized. *Nothing can be further from the truth!*

I refer you to what Jesus said to the thief on the cross. "And Jesus said unto him, Verily I say unto thee, Today shalt thou be with me in paradise" (Luke 23:43).

I don't know about you, but I don't think that man had a chance to be baptized before he died!

I will refer you to another passage, then leave it at that. Listen carefully to what Paul says to the Corinthians in 1 Corinthians 1:17: "For Christ sent me not to baptize, but to preach the gospel: not with wisdom of words, lest the cross of Christ should be made of none effect."

Here is the greatest soul winner on the planet saying that God did *not* send him to baptize. Now you would think that if salvation were dependent on water baptism, *everyone* Paul led to Christ would have been baptized.

Beloved, baptism is a skit. It is an outward expression (blue) of an inward condition (red). An illustration of what it means to be in Christ. It is you showing in visible form to your family and friends what happened to you invisibly the day you received Christ as your Savior. That day, you were baptized with His Spirit.

When I as the pastor put you under water, (this is why sprinkling does not accurately portray this), it is a picture of the death of Christ. When I hold you down for twenty minutes (only kidding), it is a picture of His burial. When I bring you up out of the water, it is a picture of His resurrection.

In Colossians 2:12, we read, "Buried with him in baptism, wherein also ye are risen with him through the faith of the operation of God, who hath raised him from the dead."

The resurrection is the key to the power of Christ over sin in our lives. The resurrection shows us that Jesus has power over *both* sin and death! When we are raised up from the water during baptism, it is symbolic of being resurrected, just as Jesus was resurrected from the tomb, in newness of life.

Being placed into Christ when we are saved is like being placed under water, completely covered. We are not seen, except through the water, just as we are not seen by God, except through Christ. We do not get baptized to be saved; we get baptized because we are saved.

Baptism is like a wedding ring. Both symbolize transactions. A wedding ring symbolizes marriage just as baptism symbolizes salvation.

Like the wedding ring, baptism signals a change in your life.

It signifies the difference between the old you and the new you. It says, "From this day forward, I stand with God."

However, wearing a wedding ring does not make you married any more than being baptized makes you saved.

Jesus is baptized into our nature so that we might be baptized into His. Jesus's baptism so identifies Him with our sin nature that the end had to take Him to the cross.

John the Baptizer had one message: you are sinners in need of forgiveness.

Beloved, apart from His voluntary self-surrender, symbolized by His baptism, all other baptisms are meaningless. Jesus has taken our sin and has been baptized for our forgiveness as a picture of the finished work of the cross!

Note that both God the Father and God the Spirit were there approving of the work of Jesus. First, the Holy Spirit descended on Jesus like a dove. The dove symbolizes purity and gentleness and peacefulness, all of which are related to Jesus.

Purity because it was not for His own sins He was baptized. Gentleness because "He would never break the bruised reed" (Isaiah 42:3). Peacefulness because His ministry brings peace between God and humans.

Remember when a dove appeared to Noah as the ark came out of the water? It was a sign of God's promise fulfilled in the deliverance from the flood of God's wrath. So the dove appears as Jesus comes out of the water as a sign of God's deliverance.

But this time the dove appears not with an olive branch in his mouth but with Jesus Himself in his grasp, as proof of God's deliverance, to which Noah pointed. So now the dove does not simply lead out one family to dry land; it leads out all who confess with their mouths and believe in their hearts!

The Spirit in the form of a dove visibly lights on Jesus, as if saying, here is the ark, which brings salvation to the world.

Then the voice of Almighty God, His Father, is heard saying so that all can hear, "You are my beloved Son; with you I am well pleased" (Mark 1:11 ESV).

God was in essence telling Jesus, "I am pleased that You were willing to leave Your glory and submit Yourself to My will even though it will lead to the cross. I am pleased that You were willing to take upon Yourself the sin of the world that the world may be saved. You are My beloved Son; with You I am well pleased."

Please understand that Jesus's baptism rebukes our sin and our self-justifications. When the water goes over Jesus's head, it is as if God is telling us sons of Adam and daughters of Eve that we are more wicked than you ever dare imagine.

We keep measuring ourselves against a broken ruler and walk away feeling we measure up. But the standard (the Law) remains unbroken. It is not really that we break the law, but the law breaks us. Then Jesus steps into the water. He who knew no sin is baptized for forgiveness. He who was high is humbled. He who created the law is judged by it.

I, Conrad, wretched man that I am, must confess I cannot even begin to understand all my sins, much less confess them. I must repent, but I do not seem to be able to. The depth of the wickedness of my heart and desires are too deep for me or any mortal to reach. I must be baptized, but the filth of my sin would only serve to get the water dirty. It will not do me any good. I would not survive the length of time I would need to spend under the water to cleanse my body, much less my soul.

It is as if Jesus is telling us, "I will get baptized in your place. I will identify with your sins." And that was to be the beginning of the end for Jesus, which would culminate at the cross as He paid for the sin of Adam and the sins of the world.

He who knew no sin … Well, I will just let brother Paul tell you himself: "For he hath made him to be sin for us, who knew no sin; that we might be made the righteousness of God in him" (2 Corinthians 5:21).

Then, immediately, the Spirit drives Jesus into the wilderness. Why? Because it simply was not enough for the last Adam to die for us; He first had to live for us. That is why I said earlier that the life He lived qualified Him to die the death He died!

Jesus lived that perfect life and showed perfect obedience by being tempted in every way yet without sin. The first Adam, in paradise, had every opportunity to succeed. Yet he rebelled and fell from paradise. The second Adam, in the desert, the wilderness, had every opportunity to fail. Yet He submitted to God and earned righteousness.

First Corinthians 10:13 says, "No temptation has overtaken you except such as is common to man; but God is faithful, who will not allow you to be tempted beyond what you are able, but with the temptation will also make the way of escape, that you may be able to bear it" (NKJV).

We are united to the first Adam by birth, and in his fall, we are condemned. But a new Adam came. We may be united to Him also, and that also by birth—not born of a woman but *born again*, this time of His Spirit.

By blue birth, we are united to Adam. By red birth, we are united to Jesus—not by water baptism but by faith alone.

❖

CHAPTER FIFTEEN

THE RAPTURE

E arly on in this book, I mentioned the Rapture. To be honest
with you, I had no intention of expounding on that subject
in this book. But since I mentioned it, let me say a few words on
the subject.

In 1 Thessalonians 4:13–18, Paul tells us not to be ignorant
concerning our brothers and sisters who have passed on.

Paul is talking about those who have died having received
Christ as Savior. He uses the words *fallen asleep*. In other words,
we close our eyes here and open them up in the presence of God
(2 Corinthians 5:8).

First Thessalonians 4:13–18 goes on to tell us about the
Rapture. We are taught in the Word to expect it at any moment,
even today. It behooves us to be ready for the day when the
church will be raptured.

You would be surprised at how many preachers today do not
believe in a literal second coming of Christ. One day, and I think
that day is not too far off, Christ will come in the air. When He
comes, the dead in Christ shall rise. Then the living Christians
will be caught up to meet Him in the air.

This will happen so fast that the Bible calls it a twinkling of an eye. This verse tells us that our vile bodies will be changed and fashioned like His glorious body—*purple*.

Here we go again. Let me explain my use of the color purple. You already know the blue and the red—blue speaking of the flesh, red speaking of the spirit.

When Jesus walked the earth, He was 100 percent red (God) and 100 percent blue (man). He was a red-filled man walking among empty blue people. He was the only red-filled man to ever walk the earth since Adam.

When He died, they buried His blue body in the tomb of Joseph of Arimathea. He committed His red Spirit to His Father: "Into thy hands I commend my spirit" (Luke 23:46)

When He resurrected, it was not just a red spirit inside and limited by a mortal blue body. It was an alloy of divinity and humanity—a mixture of the body and the spirit.

Now when you take red and mix it with blue, what color do you get? Exactly! Purple! What better picture of the glorified body of Christ after His resurrection than the royal color purple.

Now, let's get back to the Rapture.

Paul called the Rapture of the church a blessed hope. I want you to understand that Jesus is literally getting ready to come back for His church. The great hope of the church is that Christ will come and rapture us to heaven before death intervenes.

However, if death comes first, at the Rapture we shall be resurrected and given glorified bodies like Jesus on the day He does return.

There are two future comings of Jesus mentioned in the Bible. The first coming will be to meet the saints in the air. The next one will be with the saints to rule on the earth.

One is called the Rapture, and the other is called the Return. His first coming in the air is to catch away the saints into heaven.

Seven years later, He will return with the saints to set up His millennial rule upon this earth.

In verse 16, Paul launches a discussion on what we call the Rapture. "For the Lord Himself will descend from heaven with a shout, with the voice of an archangel, and with the trumpet of God. And the dead in Christ will rise first" (NKJV).

Now, the word *Rapture* is not found in the Bible. The word Rapture is not there, but the word *perusia* is, which means "to literally snatch away," "to catch up," "to come down and remove forcefully" those who are ready to meet the Lord in the air.

Paul wanted the people in Thessalonica to realize that Jesus Himself would return, not someone else.

It would be the same Jesus who walked along the shores of Galilee. Acts 1:11 records, "This same Jesus, which is taken up from you into heaven, shall so come in like manner as ye have seen him go into heaven."

Have you noticed that every time Jesus shouts, a resurrection takes place? Remember when He shouted, "Lazarus, come forth"? Suddenly, His friend Lazarus, who had been dead for four days, came forth (John 11:43–44 NKJV).

Please understand that had Jesus just said, "Come forth!" and not called Lazarus by name, every dead thing within the sound of His voice would have come forth!

The next time Jesus shouted was on Mount Calvary. Matthew 27:50–53 tells us that after Jesus had been on the cross for six hours, He shouted, "It is finished." And the graves of many who had passed away were opened, and they were seen walking around Jerusalem in their resurrected bodies. At that instant, many bodies of saints came out of their graves and returned alive to Jerusalem.

When Jesus returns in the air to catch away all believers, there will not just be one person like Lazarus or the hundreds like when He shouted from the cross, but millions from every nation, tribe, and tongue who have died in Christ and who are alive when He comes.

In John 5:28–29, the Bible says, "The hour is coming in which all that are in the graves shall hear his voice, and shall come forth."

If you don't know the voice of Jesus now, you will be left behind.

The Bible says that "the Lord Himself will descend from heaven with a shout, with the voice of the archangel, and with the trumpet of God. And the dead in Christ will rise first" (1 Thessalonians 4:16 NKJV).

After the Rapture of the church, God will take up with Israel where He left off nearly two thousand years ago.

Beloved, it could happen at any time. It will signal a time of evil, the likes of which we can't even begin to imagine. "For then shall be great tribulation, such as was not since the beginning of the world to this time, no, nor ever shall be" (Matthew 24:21).

Satan does not have a free reign now, but he will have it then. Once the church is taken away and the saints are raptured or resurrected, there will be seven years of terror, pestilence, famine, and destruction as the forces of evil battle against the nation of Israel.

It will signal the rule of Antichrist, idolatry, humanism, persecution, the worship of humankind, deception, death, and destruction. It will be the most terrible time in the history of humankind because the church will be gone.

You need to be prepared now for the coming of Jesus Christ.

Are you prepared should Jesus return today?

❖

CHAPTER SIXTEEN

CLOSING COMMENTS

First, I want to thank you for honoring me and reading this book. I pray that you were not only informed but also blessed. I hope that you enjoyed it enough to tell others about it, especially any loved one or friend who may not know the Lord. Please keep my family and me in your prayers.

Let me leave you with this blessing ...

The LORD bless you, and keep you; The LORD make His face shine upon you, and be gracious to you; The LORD lift up His countenance upon you, and give you peace. (Numbers 6:24–26)

And that is all I have to say about that!

Printed in the United States
by Baker & Taylor Publisher Services